PREJUDICE AND PROPERTY

PREJUDICE AND PROPERTY

An Historic Brief Against Racial Covenants

SUBMITTED TO THE SUPREME COURT

By TOM C. CLARK
Attorney General of the U. S.

AND

PHILIP B. PERLMAN
Solicitor General of the U. S.

U. S. Dept of Justice

GREENWOOD PRESS, PUBLISHERS
NEW YORK

Originally published in 1948, Washington, D.C.

First Greenwood Reprinting 1969

Library of Congress Catalogue Card Number 75-90725

SBN 8371-2221-X

INTRODUCTION

Why is the law so difficult to understand? It shouldn't be. This historic brief in the restrictive covenants cases shows that it needn't be.

Intentionally or otherwise, the law has been burdened with such a welter of esoteric jargon and procedural hocus-pocus that it has become far removed from the realities of life as the average person knows them. Small wonder, then, that laymen are increasingly coming to the conclusion that there is something profoundly wrong with the law.

The gap of understanding should be bridged. The lack of intelligibility, the confusion of the law, must end. The translation of legalese into plain English, legal precedents into historical facts, and legal principles into everyday observations is long overdue. The people should be let in on the law. It's their business.

There are few who would argue today that laymen should not be allowed to read the Bible, yet it was not so long ago that clergymen claimed exclusive authority over its contents and interpretation. The law will also gain from lay reading and understanding.

Take restrictive covenants as an example—an excellent example. The pure scholar of the law may refer to these strange real estate agreements as "incorporeal hereditaments." The practicing attorney will not go quite this far, perhaps because he has forgotten the expression; but he will go so far as to point out that there is a "covenant running with the land." Only a few would be so blunt—and unprofessional—as to come right out and explain that there is a clause in your ownership papers which prevents you from selling your property to Negroes, Chinese, Jews, and a host of other minority groups whom someone back in the chain of ownership didn't like.

The very generous lawyer may go on to explain that this clause operates just like those which keep many owners from building right up against the sidewalk, from piling garbage in the front yard or from raising goats on the premises.

After the strictures and mysteries of legal form are put aside, one reaches the matter of substance. Ask what your restrictive covenant means and you will be told that it stipulates that you can sell your property only to white people of certain qualifications and that this is binding on you even though it was not your idea.

From this point on is where the law and its practitioners have the best chance to be of more service to the people than they've been. The chance is missed far too often.

This brief is a major exception. The lawyers who prepared it deal with the real meaning of restrictive covenants. They draw clear-cut distinctions between human beings and building lines. For light on the effect of covenants, they checked with the people who know about such matters at first hand. They read studies by experts who are not lawyers. Out of the wealth of information they compiled came this significant document.

It is difficult to exaggerate the importance of the legal cases which moved the Justice Department to prepare this brief. The fundamental question at stake is whether the courts should enforce real estate agreements that bar a man—a fellow citizen —from occupying this house or that because of the color of his skin or the nature of his religious beliefs. Surprisingly enough, this private legal system was not put squarely before the Supreme Court until this year.

Fundamentally, there is a deep conflict here between human and property rights. The cases involved are of such profound importance that they have been aptly compared with the Dred Scott case concerning legal rights of slaves—a case which went to the heart of the issue precipitating the Civil War.

The mere fact that the Justice Department filed this brief with the Supreme Court, even though the federal government is not a party to the covenant cases submitted to that tribunal, illustrates that some progress is being made toward letting the people in on the law. But the door is merely ajar. It should be opened wider.

Something must be done to make legal documents more easily available. As things now stand, such documents are beyond the reach of the average library, let alone the average person. Were it not for the public service of the publisher of "Prejudice and Property," this brief, for example, would probably be gathering dust in the files of a dozen lawyers and judges.

The situation is particularly serious in connection with those cases in which the Justice Department submits a brief *amicus curiae, as* "friend of the court," which it is doing more frequently. Filing of such a brief recognizes the public interest in the case, yet the public doesn't really get in on it.

Making the arguments more widely available will help considerably, but other improvements are necessary. Corporations have recognized the necessity of making their annual reports readable; the government has a similar obligation to its stockholders. Within the confines of legal requirements, this particular brief goes far to meet that end—particularly since the publisher has deftly arranged the material in a convenient and attractive manner and has placed all of the citations and references at the back of the book. The result is something between a document and a story of unusual significance. An excellent precedent has been set.

WESLEY McCUNE
Washington, D. C.

CONTENTS

I: RACIAL RESTRICTIVE COVENANTS

Racial covenants, prohibiting sale to or occupancy of designated real property by certain minority groups, had only sporadic existence before the great twin migration of Negroes, in the second decade of this century, from the country to the cities in both North and South, and from the South to the Northern and Middle Western States.[1] This extensive migration first led to efforts to insure urban residential segregation by means of state or municipal legislation—beginning with a Baltimore ordinance of 1910, which was quickly followed by Atlanta, Richmond, Louisville, and other cities—until this method was completely invalidated, in 1917, in *Buchanan v. Warley*.[2] It was then that the racial covenant, which had been developing as a subsidiary weapon, became the primary legal means of enforcing segregation.[3] The course of covenant litigation since 1917 suffices by itself to show that racial restrictive agreements have come into common and increasing use since that time.[4]

In form, these covenants restrict either (a) sale, lease, conveyance to, or ownership by, any member of an excluded group or (b) use or occupancy by any member of that group, or (c) both ownership and use or occupancy. In those states invalidating group restrictions on sale or ownership under the common-law rule on restraints against alienation, the agreement usually refers only to "use' 'or "occupancy;"[5] in the other jurisdictions, outright restraints on sale or conveyance appear to be more common. Some of the covenants are limited in duration, while others are perpetual.

These variations are well illustrated by the restrictions in the four cases at bar. In the District of Columbia cases, the covenant is not limited in time and runs against sale or ownership; it provides "that said lot shall never be rented, leased, sold, transferred or conveyed unto any Negro or colored person."[6] In the Michigan case, the covenant runs until January 1, 1960, and relates only to use or occupancy: "This property shall not be used or occupied by any person or persons except those of the Caucasian race."[7] The restriction in the Missouri case runs for fifty years from February, 1911, and is likewise phrased to exclude "use" and "occupancy" by persons "not of the Caucasian race."[8] Racial restrictions are sometimes inserted in deeds,[9] but often[10] are embodied in written agreements between a group of neighborhood land-owners, which are then officially recorded so as to give due notice to all subsequent purchasers or occupants. Enforcement of the restriction is usually by a neighboring owner who is a party to such a recorded agreement, or who may assert an interest in the restriction under the rules normally governing covenants running with the land. Almost invariably the relief requested is the removal of the excluded occupant, or injunction against his entry, and, where sale restrictions have been violated, cancellation of the offending deeds.

Racial Covenants and Negro Housing

Two of the notorious social facts of American life are that Negroes suffer from deplorably inadequate housing, and that in urban areas they live, in general, in segregated zones. "Nothing is so obvious about the Negroes' level of living as the fact that most of them suffer from poor housing conditions. It is a matter of such common knowledge that it does not need much emphasis."[11] Poverty is, of course, a major cause for the dilapidated, overcrowded, unsanitary, and inadequate homes in which the mass of colored people now live, but it is residential segregation in severely limited areas which accentuates these conditions and bars their alleviation.

Increase in Negro Urban Population in the United States

	1910	1920	1930	1940
Number of Negroes urbanized	2,684,797	3,559,473	5,193,913	6,253,588
Percentage of Negroes urbanized	27.3	34.0	43.7	48.6
Percentage of total United States population urbanized	45.8	51.4	56.2	56.5

Increase in Negro Population in Ten Leading Industrial Cities

City	1940		1910		1920		1930	
	Number of Negroes	% of total pop.	Number of Negroes	% of total pop.	Number of Negroes	% of total pop.	Number of Negroes	% of total pop.
New York	91,709	1.9	152,467	2.7	327,706	4.7	458,444	6.1
Chicago	44,103	2.0	109,458	4.1	233,903	6.9	277,731	8.2
Philadelphia	84,459	5.5	134,229	7.4	219,599	11.3	250,880	13.0
Detroit	5,741	1.2	40,838	4.1	120,066	7.7	149,119	9.2
Cleveland	8,448	1.5	34,451	4.3	71,899	8.0	84,504	9.6
St. Louis	43,960	6.4	69,854	9.0	93,580	11.4	108,765	13.3
Pittsburgh	25,623	4.7	37,725	6.4	54,983	8.2	62,216	9.3
Cincinnati	19,639	5.1	30,079	7.5	47,818	10.6	55,593	12.2
Indianapolis	21,816	9.3	34,678	11.0	43,967	12.1	51,142	13.2
Kansas City, Mo.	23,556	9.5	30,719	9.5	38,574	9.8	41,574	10.4

Since the turn of the century, Negroes have been streaming to the cities (especialy in the North and Middle West—and, since World War II, to the Far West), to be faced by residential segregation, enforced by informal and formal pressures and by legal and illegal methods, which keeps them from normal expansion into "non-colored" urban areas to satisfy their housing needs.[13] The result of this bottling-up of an ever-increasing Negro population within narrow confines of colored zones or ghettos has been the abnormal over-crowding, congestion, and substandard facilities stigmatized by the President's Committee on Civil Rights and by all students of Negro housing, and so graphically portrayed in the materials presented by petitioners, as well as by Justice Edgerton.[14] As far back as 1932, the Report on Negro Housing of the President's Conference on Home Building and Home Ownership found that segregation "has kept the Negro-occupied sections of the cities throughout the country fatally unwholesome places, a menace to the health, morals, and general decency of cities and ·plague spots for race exploitations, fric-

tion and riots.' "[15]   The passing of fifteen years—which have
included the depression period, the war years, and the current
acute housing shortage—has not served to weaken the sound-
ness of his judgment.[16]

It is perhaps almost superfluous to add that, as the 1932
Report indicates, the combination of inadequate housing with
racial segregation has most unfortunate economic, social, and
psychological effects.   Colored people are forced to pay higher
rents and housing costs by the semi-monopoly which segregation fosters.[17]   The incidence of crime and juvenile delinquency
is much greater[18] and the occurrence of death and disease
among Negroes is substantially increased.[19]   And to the
corrosion which such congested and inadequate living conditions work upon any poorly housed individual's mental health,
as a citizen and human being, there must be added the pecu-
liarly disintegrating acid which enforced segregation distills
to harm not only the victim alone, but the whole fabric of
American life.[20]

Function of Racial Covenants in Enforcing Segregation

Racial covenants have a dominant role in maintaining and
enforcing this pattern of Negro residential segregation.   In the
first place, the wholesale use, in recent years, of racial restrictions, and artificially removes from availability for Negroes
who can afford to move into a city's suburbs or outlying sections, and artificially removes from availability for Negroes
large areas open to satisfy the housing needs of the rest of the
city's expanding population.   More importantly, covenants
have frequently been used to fringe the established colored
area, or "Black Belt," and thus prevent normal expansion within the already built-up portions of the city.[22]

Chicago, the home of the most intense covenant activity, is
perhaps the clearest example, with the existing Negro areas

hemmed in by a band of restrictive agreements, or by commercial and industrial properties.[23] In Los Angeles, with the coming of large numbers of Negroes during the war, there was a "veritable wave of covenantry" in new subdivisions, and in sections surrounding existing colored settlements.[24] According to the National Association for the Advancement of the Colored People,[25] covenants in St. Louis and Philadelphia are likewise strategically located so as to prevent Negroes' entry into vacant land, new subdivisions, or to most established residential areas contiguous to existing colored communities; in Detroit, the use of covenants is more recent, but even now a large part of the houses which would appeal to Negroes because of location or cost are excluded from their occupancy.[26] The American Council on Race Relations makes a similar report as to Columbus, Ohio, a city with a high incidence of exclusionary covenants. In New York City, it is likely that new areas in such expanding portions of the city as the Borough of Queens, and in the suburbs, are effectively closed to Negro occupancy.[27] In the District of Columbia, as in other cities, the present aggregate of restricted areas is not accurately known, but it seems certain that most of the "new building sites and many older areas are now covenanted" against Negroes[28]; and reports in the daily press of recent months indicate that vigorous efforts to increase the restricted portions of the city are continuing. In 1929, it was reported that the racial covenant "seems to be the most widely employed method for keeping Negroes out of 'exclusively white' residential districts."[29]

Governmental agencies concerned with housing, drawing upon their recent experience, buttress the conclusion that racial restrictive agreements have had widespread use in preventing proper expansion and development of Negro housing. The letter of the present Administrator of the Housing and Home Finance Agency, quoted above,[30] states that his agency's field reports "reveal the increasing application of these deed re-

strictions during recent years," and cites "repeated reports of
the inability of private developers to locate adequate building
sites uncovenanted and open to occupancy by Negroes, Latin-
Americans, Asiatics, and other similar groups." During the
war, John B. Blandford, first Administrator of the National
Housing Agency, stated publicly that "the problems of site
selection and racial restrictive covenants" are "barriers which
exist even for the Negro citizen who can pay for a home, and,
if permitted, could raise a family in decent surrounding."[31]
Wilson W. Wyatt, former National Housing Expediter and
successor to Mr. Blandford as Administrator of the National
Housing Agency, likewise stated that "All of us know that
because of neighborhood resistance and restrictions upon the
use of land, new home sites—one of the keys to the problem
—often are difficult to acquire for minority groups. During
the war these restrictions too many times delayed or completely
blocked private and public efforts to produce essential housing
for minority group war workers."[32] The National Housing
Agency's Conference for Racial Relations Advisers[33] stated:
"Because of racial restrictive covenants and other discriminatory practices, heavy concentrations of Negroes in limited
areas are typical in communities where there are large proportions of Negro population. In usual patterns of urban
growth, congestion is relieved somewhat by decentralization
in which people move to outlying areas. Not so with Negroes.
Their mobility is sharply limited . . . Large scale builders
indicate that even where contractors appreciate the market
for privately financed housing among Negroes and have adequate financing resources readily available, they are often
stymied by lack of unrestricted or unopposed building sites."

The significance of racial covenants in confining Negroes'
housing within tightly limited areas has likewise been stressed
by unofficial students of the general problem of racial residential segregation. The comprehensive survey of Gunnar

Myrdal, and his associates, recognizes that if private restrictive agreements were not enforceable, "segregation in the North would be nearly doomed, and segregation in the South would be set back slightly."[34]

At times of severe general housing shortages throughout the country, like the present, restrictive covenants directed against Negroes have a specially disastrous impact. Even in more normal times, segregation tends to raise rents in the colored zones and forces overcrowding and acceptance of ramshackle housing,[35] but a period of general housing scarcity simultaneously increases both the resistance of whites against Negro expansion outward and the pressure within the colored areas to burst out of confinement.

As Justice Edgerton put the matter: "Covenants prevent free competition for a short supply of housing and curtail the supply available to Negroes. They add an artificial and special scarcity to a general scarcity, particularly where the number and purchasing power of Negroes as well as whites have increased as they have recently in the District of Columbia. The effect is qualitative as well as quantitative. Exclusion from decent housing confines Negroes to slums to an even greater extent than their poverty makes necessary. Covenants exclude Negroes from a large fraction—no one knows just how large—of the decent housing in the District of Columbia. Some of it is within the economic reach of some of them. Because it is beyond their legal reach, relatively well-to-do Negroes are compelled to compete for inferior housing in unrestricted areas, and so on down the economic scale. That enforced housing segregation, in such circumstances, increases crowding squalor, and prices in the areas where Negroes are compelled to live is obvious."[36]

Current Trends in Use of Racial Covenants

We have outlined the present incidence and effect of covenants excluding occupation of Negroes, the minority group
suffering most from residential restrictions.[37]   Records also
exist of substantial use of racial covenants against Mexicans,
Armenians, Chinese, Japanese, Jews, Persians, Syrians, Filipinos, American Indians, other "non-Caucasians," or "colored
persons."[38]   And the unmistakable trend is toward increasing
use of the racial covenant, primarily against Negroes but also,
with accelerating expansion, against other minorities.

The best available information is that the great bulk of new
urban subdivisions and real estate developments which have
been commenced since residential building was resumed after
World War II are restricted, at least in those regions in which
minorities reside.   The same is probably true, though to a
lesser degree, of residential developments planned and built
in the decade before the war brought an abrupt halt to housing
construction; and since 1920 the trend toward use of racial
exclusions in new developments appears to have been steadily
upward, both within those urban and suburban areas in which
this method of residential segregation was originally used,
and also in extension to previously untouched cities.[39]

If this trend continues unchecked, almost all new residential sections of our cities will be barred, within ten or
twenty years, from occupancy by Negroes, and to an increasing
degree by other groups.   In those communities, like Washington, in which Negroes are seeking escape from desperate
overcrowding in the traditional colored areas by purchasing
houses in existing "white neighborhoods," there has been a
noticeable tendency to prevent the "invasion" by the intense
promotion, signing, and recording of new restrictions in those
old areas, as well as by more informal methods.   The result
is that "where old ghettos are surrounded by restrictions, and

new subdivisions are also encumbered by them, there is practically no place for the people against whom the restrictions are directed to go."[40]

The Present Legal Status of Racial Restrictive Covenants

Courts in some nineteen states, and the District of Columbia, have indicated that racial restrictive covenants of one type or another are enforceable, and 'in no jurisdiction have they been entirely invalidated, though there are at least two reported lower court expressions of unconstitutionality.[41] The earliest case involving Negroes was decided in Louisiana in 1915, but all the other decisions have issued since this Court's holding, in November 1917, that state or muncipal residential segregation violated the Fourteenth Amendment.[42]

Since 1918, the highest courts of Alabama, California, Colorado, Georgia, Kansas, Kentucky, Louisiana, Maryland, Michigan, Missouri, North Carolina, Oklahoma, Texas, West Virginia, and Wisconsin, as well as the Court of Appeals for the District of Columbia, have held, or clearly stated in dictum, that racial restraints, properly phrased, would be enforced; a recent Ohio Court of Appeals case, three lower New York courts, a New Jersey *nisi prius* decision, and apparently a decision of the Illinois Appellate Court, are in accord.[43] The other twenty-nine states are silent. The two dissenting voices are those of District Judge Erskine M. Ross, who held, in 1892, in the first reported American case in this field, that enforcement of a covenant against renting to "a Chinaman" would be unconstitutional,[44] and of a New Jersey vice-chancellor who stated *obiter* the unconstitutionality of covenants excluding Jews.[45]

Most of the cases sustaining the enforcement of racial agreements or conditions have dismissed constitutional objections with no more than a reference to *Corrigan* v. *Buckley*,[46] which is widely but erroneously regarded as settling the issue.[47] In the others, consideration of constitutional questions has been left with the bald conclusion that the Fourteenth Amendment protects only against "state action"[48] or with the intimation that the discrimination is of the type permissible under the Constitution.[49]

In some jurisdictions, the cases discuss the validity of racial exclusions under the common-law rule forbidding restraints on alienation, but in those states in which restraints on sales or leases are held void at common law, similar racial restrictions on use or occupancy are upheld.[50] The equity of affirmatively enforcing restrictions against Negroes or other minority groups gravely in need of housing space has hardly been touched;[51] but public policy barriers to validity of the covenants have been mooted in many cases, only to meet with short judicial rejection.[52]

Some mitigation of the harsh effects of racial covenants is found in the rule, in several jurisdictions, that the agreements will not be enforced where infiltration of the excluded group has caused such a change in the neighborhood that it would be to the pecuniary advantage of the property owners to remove the restriction and permit them to sell outside the restriction.[53] However, even this rule is narrowly construed by some courts, including those of the District of Columbia; in order to protect owners who desire to remain.[54]

This Court has thrice voided legislative attempts at racial residential segregation as violative of the Fourteenth Amendment. In *Buchanan* v. *Warley*,[55] the Court annulled an ordinance of Louisville, Kentucky, which prohibited either white or colored persons from occupying houses in blocks in which the majority of houses were occupied by persons of the other race. A *per curiam* memorandum in *Harmon* v. *Tyler*,[56] invalidated, on the authority of the *Buchanan* case, a New Orleans ordinance forbidding white or colored persons from establishing residence in a Negro or white community, respectively, "except on the written consent of a majority of the persons of the opposite race inhabiting such community or portion of the city." The third case, *City of Richmond* v. *Deans*,[57] rested on the two earlier decisions in holding invalid a Richmond ordinance prohibiting "any person from using as a residence any building on any street between intersecting streets where the majority of residences on such street are occupied by those with whom said person is forbidden to intermarry" by Virginia law. State courts have likewise refused enforcement to legislative ordinances or statutes restricting or regulating sale or occupancy of residences on a racial basis.[58]

The one case in this Court directly involving racial restrictive agreements is *Corrigan* v. *Buckley*,[59] in which *appeal* from the Court of Appeals' decision[60] was dismissed for want of jurisdiction on the ground that a contention that the covenants were "void" *ab initio* under the Fifth, Thirteenth, and Fourteenth Amendments, and the Civil Rights statutes, raised no substantial constitutional or statutory issue. No question of the constitutional validity of judicial enforcement of the covenants was properly before the Court, and issues of the common-law legality of the restraint or of equitable discretion in enforcement were not considered.[61]

In Canada, the Ontario High Court has held racial and religious restrictive agreements invalid under provincial and Dominion public policy, as well as void restraints at common law.[62] We have found no English or Australian cases on the point.[63]

II: THE NATION'S RESPONSIBILITIES

The Federal Government has a special responsibility for the protection of the fundamental civil rights guaranteed to the people by the Constitution and laws of the United States. The President of the United States recently stated:

"We must make the Federal Government a friendly vigilant defender of the rights and equalities of all Americans. . . . Our National Government must show the way."[1]

The Government is of the view that judicial enforcement of racial restrictive covenants on real property is incompatible with the spirit and letter of the Constitution and laws of the United States. It is fundamental that no agency of government should participate in any action which will result in depriving any person of essential rights because of race or color or creed.

This Court has held that such discriminations are prohibited by the organic law of the land, and that no legislative body has power to create them. It must follow, therefore, that the Constitutional rights guaranteed to every person cannot be denied by private contracts enforced by the judicial branch of government—especially where the discriminations created by private contracts have grown to such proportions as to become detrimental to the public welfare and against public policy.

Residential restrictions based on race, color, ancestry, or religion have become a familiar phenomenon in almost every large community of this country, affecting the lives, the health, and the well-being of millions of Americans. Such restrictions are not confined to any single minority group. While

Negroes (of whom there are approximately 13 million in the United States) have suffered most because of such discriminations, restrictive covenants have also been directed against Indians, Jews, Chinese, Japanese, Mexicans, Hawaiians, Puerto Ricans, Filipinos, and "non-Caucasians."

This nation was founded upon the declaration that all men are endowed by their Creator with certain inalienable rights, and that among these rights are life, liberty and the pursuit of happiness. To that declaration was added the Fifth Amendment of the Bill of Rights, providing that no person shall be deprived of life, liberty or property without due process of law; and the Fourteenth Amendment, providing that no State shall deprive any person of life, liberty or property, without due process of law, nor deny to any person within its jurisdiction the equal protection of the laws. And Congress, exercising its power to enforce the provisions of the Fourteenth Amendment, has provided that all citizens of the United States shall have the same right, in every State and Territory, as is enjoyed by white citizens to inherit, purchase, lease, sell, hold, and convey real and personal property.

Racial restrictive covenants on real property are of comparatively recent origin. If limited in number, and confined to insignificant areas, they would not have been of such public importance. But they have already expanded in large cities from coast to coast. They are responsible for the creation of isolated areas in which overcrowded racial minorities are confined, and in which living conditions are steadily worsened. The avenues of escape are being narrowed and reduced. As to the people so trapped, there is no life in the accepted sense of the word; liberty is a mockery, and the right to pursue happiness a phrase without meaning, empty of hope and reality. This situation cannot be reconciled with the spirit of mutual tolerance and respect for the dignity and rights of the individual which give vitality to our democratic way of life.

The time has come to destroy these evils which threaten the safety of our free institutions.

The fact that racial restrictive covenants are being enforced by instrumentalities of government has become a source of serious embarrassment to agencies of the Federal Government in the performance of many essential functions, including the programs relating to housing and home finance, to public health, to the protection of dependent native racial minorities in the United States and its territories, to the conduct of foreign affairs, and to the protection of civil rights.

Housing

The Administrator of the Housing and Home Finance Agency has prepared the following statement describing the effects which the widespread use of racial restrictive covenants has had upon the operations of that agency:

"Racial restrictive covenants, as the core of a system of traditional real estate practices controlling the access of Negroes and other racial minority groups to sites and dwelling units, have affected practically every phase of public housing administration during the past thirteen years. By generally restricting these groups to sharply defined neighborhoods which provide too few houses and too little living space, these covenants have served to distort the objectives of the public housing program. The ultimate effect of covenanted land restrictions is to place the Federal agency, required as it is to clear and replace slum areas, in the position of appearing to place the stamp of government approval upon separate residential patterns and to render it most difficult for the agency to administer public funds in such manner as to assure equitable participation by minority racial groups.

"As a result, administrative problems arise to confront the agency at every stage of the program—the programming of projects and dwelling units, determination of sites, acquisition and assembly of land, provision of project services and facilities, general project management and disposition. The processes involved not only impede the progress of the program, in many instances, but are often excessive in cost and thereby reduce the total amount of housing and facilities which might otherwise be provided with the funds available.

"Inasmuch as the local approach to housing is generally conditioned by the patterns maintained by racial restrictive covenants, the earliest stages of planning with local housing authorities to meet the housing needs of racial segments in the low-rent market on an equitable basis must include racial breakdowns and anticipate location and occupancy conditions accordingly.

"The most serious distortion of planning occurs at the site selection stages at which sites offered by the local authority must be evaluated in terms of the racial composition of the prospective project occupants. In many communities, racial minority groups are land-bound within areas restricted by the existence of racial covenants on undeveloped as well as developed areas. The result is excessive overcrowding in the slum and blighted areas with which the basic purposes of the low-rent public housing program are concerned. Repercussions upon the program are extensive. Obstacles to the location of racial minorities outside of the areas to which they are restricted necessitate site selection for developments to house such groups within these inordinately overcrowded areas. At the same time, the excessive overcrowding tends to increase the cost of the land. Moreover, there is the danger of increasing the density of other restricted and overcrowded areas which must absorb the racial minority group families temporarily or permanently displaced from similar areas by public housing developments. In many cases, alternative housing cannot be provided at all without demolition of units already occupied and desperately needed as the only shelter available to the racial minority groups.

"While these conditions would naturally constitute a part of the inevitable problems to be dealt with by a program limited to unit for unit replacement, the degree of hardship and the limitation of sound solutions are far greater when racial minority groups are involved.

"When open sites are sought or used under such circumstances as the need for lower cost land, relieving the congestion of the slum area, avoiding displacement of more units than the program can replace under acceptable density standards, or the requirements of the war housing program, objections to use of such sites for housing to which racial minorities will be admitted are frequently obstructive and sometimes prohibitive. An outstanding example of the local, national and even international implications involved is the development of the Sojourner Truth project in Detroit, Michigan, which the Department of Justice investigated incident to the violence which accompanied the moving of Negroes into this project developed on open land. The cost of this experience to national unity and international prestige is incalculable.

"Actual increased financial costs are incurred not only in the additional administrative processes required to effect suitable participation by racial groups in the program under the conditions aggravated by racial restrictive covenants, but also in the uneconomic development and administration of dual facilities and services. In the instance of Buffalo, an additional half million dollars was required to rehouse displaced Negro families from a slum site to allow the development of a project for essential Negro war workers on the only site locally available to minority group occupancy.

"Regulations . . . require local housing authorities to give eviction notices to families which have become ineligible for continued occupancy of low-rent housing projects because of increases in their income since their original admission. Negro families whose incomes now exceed the maximum limit for continued occupancy have a great deal of difficulty in finding other housing because large areas are closed to them by restrictive covenants. Furthermore, local housing authorities encounter almost unanimous resistance from the Negro community and its press, seriously impairing the type of public relations essential to the successful administration of the eviction policy. The protests place the PHA and the local authority in an almost indefensible position because of the difficulties of refuting the claims that the Negro evictees are virtually barred from competing in the open housing market for shelter on the same basis as other evicted tenants in similar economic position.

"After March 1, 1948, it will become necessary to evict such over-income families whether or not other housing accommodations have been specifically located for particular families. In addition, over 46,000 minority group families are now living in temporary war housing which must be removed by July 25, 1949, in order to comply with the legislation under funds which were provided for their construction. This is anticipated as a major problem on the West Coast where thousands of Negro war migrant families are housed in temporary projects.

"Under both of these conditions where evictions will be effected, the existence of racial restrictive covenants will probably cause a disproportionate number of Negro tenants to move from low-rent housing projects into slum areas. When such removals occur, racial minorities tend to charge the Federal Government with forcing them into situations where they suffer inequitable and discriminatory treatment.

"The disposition of permanent war housing will, of course, conform generally with the local real estate practices which are conditioned by the racial restrictive covenants. Under these local conditions, the agencies of the Federal Government responsible for the disposition program are subject to embarrassing involvement in cases where racial minority group veterans may be denied acquisition of houses to which, otherwise, they would have preference.

"These are but a few illustrations of the impact of the restrictive processes upon the operations of the PHA program. To meet these and associated problems, it has been necessary to evolve specific administrative machinery and a body of policy and procedure in order to effect a measure of equitable participation by minority racial groups. . . .

"While this subject is under study in the Agency, comprehensive and conclusive information on the extent of such covenants is not now available: Field reports, however, from such localities as Los Angeles, Chicago, Detroit, St. Louis, Baltimore, New York City and Washington, D. C., reveal the increasing application of these deed restrictions during recent years. This acknowledged fact is reflected in:

"a. The multiplicity of court actions regarding racial covenants in those cities.

"b. Repeated reports of the inability of private developers to locate adequate building sites uncovenanted and open to occupancy by Negroes, Latin-Americans, Asiatics and other similar groups.

"c. Planning commission reports on the restriction of 20 per cent of the population (Negro) of Baltimore to 2 per cent of the land areas; a density of 80,000 persons per square mile in portions of the Negro South Side in Chicago as compared to an average population density in blighted areas of 40,000; concentration of 3,871 Negroes in the famous 'lung block' in New York City's Harlem—at such density rate, all the people in the United States could be accommodated in one-half of the New York City land area. . . .

"Covenants of this type have complicated the administration of governmental housing programs throughout the past decade and have made difficult the equitable use of public funds and powers. The enforcement of such covenants provides official state support for the traditional real estate and financial practice of restricting Negroes and other racial minorities to sharply defined neighborhoods which provide too little space for expanding population groups.

"Hemmed in by these covenants, these areas have become highly congested, over-used, under-serviced and largely substandard. As a result the program of FHA mortgage insurance can have but limited application in such areas for purely economic reasons. The existence of such covenants outside these constricted areas, makes it inordinately difficult and often impossible for prospective Negro buyers to quality for FHA mortgage insurance. As a result, the middle income market among Negroes and similar racial minorities is largely excluded from the benefits of the mortgage insurance program.

"Land restrictions are a primary factor in the minority housing market, which results in higher costs of credit and disproportionately limits the purchasing power of the housing dollar of minority groups. This indirectly affects the extent to which minority groups benefit from state or federally aided financing operations.

"Court enforced racial covenants disproportionately limit the occupied neighborhoods and open areas available for the development of public housing projects open to minority group occupancy. Thus the federal public housing program experiences serious administrative difficulties in efforts to meet the disproportionately large mass housing market among minority group low-income families.

"Local, state or federal programs offering aid to land assembly, urban redevelopment and community facilities are hampered by such covenants.

"The resultant inequity in the expenditure of public funds and the compulsion upon federal agencies to conform to "community patterns" render federal housing agencies subject to the double charge of placing the stamp of governmental approval upon residential segregation and administering the funds or powers of all the people in a discriminatory manner."[2]

Public Health

The Surgeon General of the United States Public Health Service has made the following statement as to the health problems which arise from the artificial quarantine of minority groups in overcrowded residential areas:

"While national housing policy does not come within the official cognizance of the U. S. Public Health Service, we do regard the provision and maintenance of a sanitary environment for all the people of the country as a major and basic element of national health policy. The sanitation and hygiene of housing, accordingly, are of great importance in relation to the objectives and programs of the Public Health Service.

"The relationship between housing and health is extremely difficult technically to assess, because there are almost inevitably associated with housing concomitant factors, such as income, food, and ability to obtain medical care and education, that have a decided bearing upon health.

"While an exact assessment cannot be made on technical grounds, there is general agreement among health authorities that housing deficient in basic sanitary facilities, structurally defective from the point of view of home accidents and protection against the elements, and improperly planned in relation to the cultural resources of the community, is a serious deterrent to improved national health.

"To the extent that racial restrictive housing covenants would deny a citizen the opportunity to provide for himself a sanitary and healthful environment, such covenants would, in my view, be prejudicial to the public health."[3]

Protection of Dependent Racial Minorities

Racial restrictive covenants have become a matter of concern to the Department of the Interior because of their impact upon the administration of Indian affairs and of the territories and insular possessions of the United States. Many types of covenants are directed against broad groups which include not only American Indians but also the majority of the peoples of the territories. This has given rise to problems which are thus described by the Under-Secretary of the Interior:

Indian Affairs

"There are now about 400,000 Indians in the United States. Of these, a substantial number live in urban areas. The implications of these restrictive covenant cases affect all of them.

"One of the main goals of the Indian Service is to aid the Indians to participate equally and fully in the life of the Nation. This purpose is frustrated when Indians attempting to settle in cities are segregated by restrictive covenants into undesirable slum areas solely because they are Indians. During World War II about 75,000 Indians left their tribal reservations. Of these, some 30,000 served in the armed forces, and about 45,000 took jobs in war industry. Many of these Indians, particularly war veterans, are eager to exchange their reservation life for city life. The present critical housing shortage has been an important factor inhibiting their ability to do so. This housing shortage is greatly emphasized for Indians by racial restrictive covenants, which are extensively imposed in most of the major cities of the nation on many of the newly constructed dwellings, almost all new residential subdivisions and on many existing residential properties. The covenants, by discriminating against them solely because they are Indians and by preventing them from securing adequate urban housing, are thus an important factor in deterring Indians from going to cities to look for employment. This not only retards their economic progress but also substantially tends to burden the United States with increased expenses in the administration of Indian affairs. Since resources on many of the reservations are inadequate, relief payments by the Government would be greater, and may continue indefinitely. . . .

"It has long been the declared policy of Congress to give Indians preference in Federal employment. Some of these statutes are: Act of June 30, 1834 (4 Stat. 735, 737); act of March 3, 1875 (18 Stat. 402, 449); act of March 1, 1883 (22 Stat. 432, 451); General Allotment Act of February 8, 1887 (24 Stat. 388, 389-90); act of August 15, 1894 (28 Stat. 286, 313); Wheeler-Howard Act of June 18, 1934 (48 Stat. 984, 986, 25 U. S. C. 472). Many other statutes are listed in F. S. Cohen, *Handbook of Federal Indian Law,* 159-162 (1945). To help the Indians achieve self-government is one of the principal aims of the Indian Service. For this reason, as well as because of their natural sympathy and understanding of Indian problems and customs, Indians are particularly suitable for employment in the Indian Service. Over 50 per cent of the employees of the Indian Service are of Indian ancestry.

"There have been a number of instances in which such Indian employees have been impeded by restrictive covenants in securing adequate housing accommodations. In at least one instance, an Indian employee who had purchased a home in the Washington, D. C., area subject to such a covenant, experienced great difficulty in securing the refund of his down-payment for his home. Inability to secure adequate housing because of restrictive covenants would be a serious deterrent to the employment of Indians in the Indian Service, and would defeat the congressional policy of preferential employment of Indians.

"Furthermore, the restrictions upon their securing adequate housing, by deterring them from remaining employed in the cities where Indian Service offices are located, may seriously jeopardize the functioning of the entire Indian Service. The impact of restrictive covenants on Indians has been a factor in the quest for homes in the Washington, D. C. area by the large number of Indian employees who have recently been transferred with the transfer of the Bureau's headquarters, from Chicago to Washington.

"The effect of restrictive covenants on the morale of all the Indians is also significant. Much of the effort to eradi-cate old injuries to Indians and to aid in their participation in the national life is stultified by their being categorized as inferior by the exclusions caused by restrictive covenants. . . .

People of the Territories and Island Possessions

"About 25 per cent of the people of Puerto Rico, one-half of the people of Alaska, most of the people in Hawaii, and about 95 per cent of the people in the Virgin Islands would be subject to classification as "non-Caucasians" and thus would be within the scope of most restrictive covenants. There is apparently no evidence that restrictive covenants are being applied against them in the territories at present; but restric-tive covenants are being applied against them in the United States and may well spread to the territories.

"Many thousands of Puerto Ricans, Hawaiians, and Virgin

Islanders are now in the United States. It has been estimated that over 350,000 Puerto Ricans are in New York City alone. Many of them live in East Harlem under appalling conditions unquestionably resulting partially from restrictive covenants.

"Restrictive covenants against these territorial peoples contribute to resentment and bitterness against the United States with consequent impairment of the Federal Government's prestige and programs in the territories. Loyalties are impaired in strategic possessions when the inhabitants of these areas find themselves categorized as second-class citizens. To the Islanders, racial discrimination is a new experience. Even the Governor of the Virgin Islands is subjected to restricted housing when he comes to the United States on official business.

"The broad implications of restrictive covenants are entirely inconsistent with the future national and international welfare of the United States in its relations with the "nonwhite" peoples. This Department firmly believes that the cancer of restrictive covenants should be excised from this nation."[4]

Conduct of Foreign Affairs

The Legal Adviser to the Secretary of State has advised that "the United States has been embarrassed in the conduct of foreign relations by acts of discrimination taking place in this country."[5] The position of the Department of State on such matters was set forth in a letter of May 8, 1946, from the then Acting Secretary of State to the Fair Employment Practices Committee:

"The existence of discrimination against minority groups in this country has an adverse effect upon our relations with other countries. We are reminded over and over by some foreign newspapers and spokesmen, that our treatment of various minorities leaves much to be desired. While sometimes these pronouncements are exaggerated and unjustified, they all too frequently point with accuracy to some form of discrimination because of race, creed, color, or national origin. Frequently we find it next to impossible to formulate a satisfatory answer to our critics in other countries; the gap between the things we stand for in principle and the facts of a particular situation may be too wide to be bridged. An atmosphere of suspicion and resentment in a country over the way a minority is being treated in the United States is a formidable obstacle to the development of mutual understanding and trust between the two countries. We will have better international relations when these reasons for suspicion and resentment have been removed.

"I think that it is quite obvious . . . that the existence of discrimination against minority groups in the United States is a handicap in our relations with other countries. The Department of State, therefore, has good reason to hope for the continued and increased effectiveness of public and private efforts to do away with these discriminations."

Protection of Civil Rights

The final and most important concern of the Government relates to its responsibility for the protection of fundamental civil rights. Without an atmosphere of mutual tolerence, civil rights cannot survive. That they shall survive is a prime objective of our system of government.

The experience of the Department of Justice in this field is, we believe, of some significance. In the enforcement of federal laws dealing with invasions of rights secured by the Constitution and laws of the United States, the Department has found in eight years of special effort that it is exceedingly difficult to redress invasions of civil rights in the face of hostile community prejudice. We have found that the most serious invasions of human liberties go hand in hand with racial intolerance.

The difficulties encountered in the enforcement of existing civil rights laws provided the impetus for the establishment on December 5, 1946, of the President's Committee on Civil Rights. No more cogent or timely statement of American ideals, and the threat to those ideals implied by the enforcement of racial restrictive covenants, could be made than that contained in the Report of this Committee, entitled *To Secure These Rights,* issued on Otober 29, 1947:

"The central theme in our American heritage is the importance of the individual person. From the earliest moment of our history we have believed that every human being has an essential dignity and integrity which must be respected and safeguarded. Moreover, we believe that the welfare of the individual is the final goal of group life. Our American heritage further teaches that to be secure in the rights he wishes for himself, each man must be willing to respect the rights of other men. This is the conscious recognition of a basic moral principle: all men are created equal as well as free. Stemming from this principle is the obligation to build social institutions that will guarantee equality of opportunity to all men. Without this equality freedom becomes an illusion. Thus the only aristocracy that is consistent with the free way of life is an aristocracy of talent and achievement. The grounds on which our society accords respect, influence or reward to each of its citizens must be limited to the quality of his personal character and of his social contribution.

"This concept of equality which is so vital a part of the American heritage knows no kinship with notions of human uniformity or regimentation. We abhor the totalitarian arrogance which makes one man say that he will respect another man as his equal only if he has, *my* race, *my* religion, *my* political views, *my* social position.' In our land men are equal, but they are free to be different. From these very differences among our people has come the great human and national strength of America.

"Thus, the aspirations and achievements of each member of our society are to be limited only by the skills and energies he brings to the opportunities equally offered to all Americans. We can tolerate no restrictions upon the individual which depend upon irrelevant factors such as his race, his color, his religion or the social position to which he is born. . . .⁶

"Equality of opportunity to rent or buy a home should exist for every American. Today, many of our citizens face a double barrier when they try to satisfy their housing needs. They first encounter a general housing shortage which makes it difficult for any family without a home to find one. They then encounter prejudice and discrimination based upon race, color, religion or national origin, which places them at a disadvantage in competing for the limited housing that is available. The fact that many of those who face this double barrier are war veterans only underlines the inadequacy of our housing record.

"Discrimination in housing results primarily from business practices. These practices may arise from special interests of business groups, such as the profits to be derived from confining minorities to slum areas, or they may reflect community prejudice. One of the most common practices is the policy of landlords and real estate agents to prevent Negroes from renting outside of designated areas. Again, it is 'good business' to develop exclusive 'restricted' suburban developments which are barred to all but white gentiles. When Negro veterans seek "GI" loans in order to build homes, they are likely to find that credit from private banks, without whose services there is no possibility of taking advantage of the GI Bill of Rights, is less freely available to members of their race. Private builders show a tendency not to construct new homes except for white occupancy. These interlocking business customs and devices form the core of our discriminatory policy. But community prejudice also finds expression in open public agitation against construction of public housing projects for Negroes, and by violence against Negroes who seek to occupy public housing projects or to build in 'white' sections."[7]

The Report also stated:

"It is impossible to decide who suffers the greatest moral damage from our civil rights transgressions, because all of us are hurt. That is certainly true of those who are victimized. Their belief in the basic truth of the American promise is undermined. But they do have the realization, galling as it sometimes is, of being morally in the right. The damage to those who are responsible for these violations of our moral standards may well be greater. They, too, have been reared to honor the command of 'free and equal.' . . . All of us must endure the cynicism about democratic values which our failures breed.

"The United States can no longer countenance these burdens on its common conscience, these inroads on its moral fiber."[8]

It is for these compelling reasons that the Government of the United States appears in these cases as *amicus curiae.*

III: CONSTITUTIONAL RIGHTS

Judicial enforcement of racial restrictive covenants constitutes governmental action in violation of rights protected by
the Constitution and Laws of the United States from discrimination on the basis of race or color.

The Government's position in these cases is based upon
the premise that the Fifth and Fourteenth Amendments are
involved only if a discrimination based on race or color (a)
is with respect to rights which under the Constitution and
laws of the United States are protected from such discrimination and (b) constitutes "federal" or "state" action within
the applicable principles laid down by this Court. We can
put to one side, therefore, acts which although involving
racial discrimination, do not run afoul of the Constitution,
either because they do not constitute governmental action or
because they do not interfere with a right which the Constitution protects from racial discrimination.

A hypothetical case may thus be distinguished: Suppose a
man refuses to sell or lease his property merely because of
the prospective purchaser's race or color. So long as his
refusal is neither sanctioned nor supported in any way by
governmental action, no constitutional question is raised. This
was decided in the *Civil Rights Cases*,[1] which held that the
Fourteenth Amendment does not prohibit racial discriminations which are merely the "wrongful acts of individuals, unsupported by state authority in the shape of laws, customs,
or judicial or executive proceedings."[2]

This phase of the argument may therefore be framed in
the following terms: (1) Does judicial enforcement of racial

restrictive covenants constitute governmental action within the applicable principles established by this Court? (2) If so, does such governmental enforcement through the judicial process constitute a denial of rights protected by the Constitution and laws of the United States?

Both these questions are clearly to be answered in the affirmative. More particularly, we contend that judicial enforcement of racial restrictive covenants constitutes governmental ation in violation of each of the following rights guaranteed by the Constitution and laws of the United States: (1) The right to acquire, use, and dispose of property, without being restricted in the exercise of such right because of race or color. (2) The right to compete on terms of equality, without being disriminated against because of race or color, in securing decent and adequate living accommodations. (3) The right to equal treatment before the law.

Judicial enforcement of private covenants constitutes governmental action.

It cannot successfully be argued that the decrees involved in these cases do not constitute governmental action because the courts have acted solely to enforce private contractual or property rights. It is well settled that ation is no less governmental because it is taken by the judicial rather than legislative or executive branches.[3]

This is true even where the judicial action is based upon common law enforcement of private rights. Thus, in *A. F. of L.* v. *Swing,* an injunction to protect an employer from an interference with his business, which under state law was tortious, was held unconstitutional as a violation of rights secured by the Fourteenth Amendment.[4] Compare *Schenectady Union Publishing Co.* v. *Sweeney,*[5] in which this Court, equally divided, affirmed a judgment for damages in a libel suit, where it was contended that such judgment infringed the freedom of speech secured by the Fourteenth Amendment. Judgments in civil cases have frequently been held unconstitutional on due process or other grounds.[6]

A court which enforces a contract is not merely a mechanical instrumentality for effectuating the will of the contracting parties. The law enforces contracts because there is a public interest in placing the force of the state behind the effectuation of private agreements not contrary to any recognized social policy. "Law is a statement of the circumstances in which the public force will be brought to bear upon men through the courts."[7] The enforcement of contracts is a *public* act involving more than the attempt of individuals to carry out their own private arrangements.

Whatever difficulties may be involved in drawing the line between governmental and individual action for other purposes, the line of demarcation is clear and precise with respect to actions involving racial discrimination. Only those actions of individuals which are in no respect sanctioned, supported, or participated in by any agency of government are beyond the scope of the Fifth and Fourteenth Amendments. Racial discriminations which are merely "the wrongful acts of individuals" can remain outside the ban of the Constitution only so long as they are "unsupported by State authority in the shape of laws, customs, or judicial or executive proceedings."[8]

The decrees below invade rights secured by the Constitution and laws of the United States.

The Scope of Constitutional Protection Against Governmental Discriminations Based on Race or Color

The decisions of this Court stand in vigorous affirmation of the principle that "our Constitution is color blind."[9] The Court has been consistent and unequivocal in its denunciation of discriminations based upon race or color.[10]

In *Hirabayashi* v. *United States*,[11] it was stated:

"Distinctions between citizens solely because of their ancestry are by their very nature odious to a free people whose institutions are founded upon the doctrine of equality. For that reason, legislative classification or discrimination based on race alone has often been held to be a denial of equal protection."[12]

The *Hirabayashi* case recognized, of course, that this principle, like all other principles of law, is not an absolute. But the attitude which the Court will take in dealing with assertedly justifiable racial restrictions was clearly defined in *Korematsu* v. *United States*. [13]

". . . all legal restrictions which curtail the civil rights of a single racial group are immediately suspect. That is not to say that all such restrictions are unconstitutional. It is to say that courts must subject them to the most rigid scrutiny. Pressing public necessity may sometimes justify the existence of such restrictions; racial antagonism never can."

The Court's approach to these questions may thus be summarized, in general terms, as follows: Distinctions based on race or color alone are in most instances irrelevant and, therefore, invidious under the Constitution. They can be justified, if at all, only by the weightiest countervailing interests. Because of its unique role in our constitutional system as the guardian of the civil rights of minorities, this Court will make the most searching inquiry into the sufficiency of any grounds asserted as justification for racial discrimination.[14] In making such inquiry, the Court will be mindful of the fact that the Fourteenth Amendment was primarily intended "to prevent state legislation designed to perpetuate discrimination on the basis of race or color."[15] While this constitutional safeguard extends to all persons alike in the rights which it secures,[16] it will not be overlooked that constitutional protection for the rights and liberties of the Negro was the primary object to be attained by adoption of the Amendment. In *Strauder* v. *West Virginia*,[17] Mr. Justice Strong's opinion for the Court stated:

"It [the Fourteenth Amendment] was designed to assure to the colored race the enjoyment of all the civil rights that under the law are enjoyed by white persons, and to give to that race the protection of the general government, in that enjoyment, whenever it should be denied by the States. . . .

"What is this but declaring that the law in the States shall be the same for the black as for the white; that all persons, whether colored or white, shall stand equal before the laws of the States, and, in regard to the colored race, for whose protection the amendment was primarily designed, that no discrimination shall be made against them by law because of their color? . . .

"The Fourteenth Amendment makes no attempt to enumerate the rights it designed to protect. It speaks in general terms, and those are as comprehensive as possible. Its language is prohibitory; but every prohibition implies the existence of rights and immunities, prominent among which is an immunity from inequality of legal protection, either for life, liberty, or property. Any State action that denies this immunity to a colored man is in conflict with the Constitution."

The Court has had occasion to apply these general principles to a variety of specific situations. The earliest class of cases involving governmental action of a discriminatory character relates to the exclusion of Negroes from juries. It was soon settled that where Negroes have been intentionally and systematically excluded from serving on a grand or petit jury, equal protection of the laws is denied to the Negro defendant against whom an indictment or conviction has been obtained. This is true whether the exclusion occurred by reason of the direct command of a state statute,[18] or because of the discriminatory practices of selection employed by state officials.[19]

Similarly, the constitutional authority given to Congress to implement the Fourteenth Amendment by appropriate legislation empowers it to provide that state officials, including judges, shall be guilty of a federal penal offense for causing such a discriminatory selection of jurors.[20]

Another class of cases involving governmental racial discriminations relates to suffrage. The right to qualify as a voter, even in primary elections, may not be denied by a State on the ground of color, without offending the equal protection clause.[21] "States may do a good deal of classifying that it is difficult to believe rational, but there are limits, and it is too clear for extended argument that color cannot be made the basis of a statutory classification affecting the right set up in this case."[22] This Court has held such discrimination unconstitutional even where it is imposed by a committee of a political party, if its authority to do so originates in the laws of the State. Mr. Justice Cardozo's opinion for the Court stated:

"Delegates of the State's power have discharged their official functions in such a way as to discriminate individiously between white citizens and black. The Fourteenth Amendment, adopted as it was with special solicitude for the equal protection of members of the Negro race, lays a duty upon the court to level by its judgment these barriers of color."

More recently, the Court has held, upon an examination of a state's statutes dealing with primaries, that the exclusion of Negroes from voting in a primary election by a political party constituted a denial by the State of the right to vote which is constitutionally secured against discrimination.[24] Even though the discrimination in that case was effected by a private organization, the Court held that where a State "endorses, adopts and enforces" the discrimination, the State itself has denied constitutional rights. The portion of the Court's opinion dealing with this question is pertinent here:

"The United States is a constitutional democracy. Its organic law grants to all citizens a right to participate in the choice of elected officials without restriction by any State because of race. This grant to the people of the opportunity for choice is not to be nullified by a State through casting its electoral process in a form which permits a private organization to practice racial discrimination in the election. Constitutional rights would be of little value if they could be thus indirectly denied."[25]

Racial discriminations prohibited by the Fourteenth Amendment are not confined solely to rights as fundamental as those relating to suffrage or to a fair criminal trial. They relate as well to the privileges which a State may offer to its citizens; what is offered to its white citizens must equally be offered to its colored citizens. To deny substantial equality in the enjoyment of such privileges is to deny the equal protection of the laws. An example is the privilege of attending the law school at a state university. A state is not required to furnish legal education to its citizens; but if it offers such education to its white citizens, an equal privilege cannot be denied to its colored citizens.[26]

A State, it has been held, may require that passengers in intrastate transportation be segregated according to color;[27] but denial of equal transportation facilities because of race or color would be a discrimination prohibited by the Constitution.[28] "The denial to appellant of equality of accommodations because of his race would be an invasion of a fundamental individual right which is guaranteed against state action by the Fourteenth Amerndment."[29]

It is also settled that the Constitution prohibits discriminations against persons of a particular race or color, which operate to prevent them from carrying on a business or calling.[30] Discrimination is no less invalid because it is evident only through the manner in which a state law is administered.

Thus, in *Yick Wo* v. *Hopkins,* it was held that equal protection of the laws was denied where city officials so administered a municipal licensing ordinance as to grant laundry permits to white persons but consistently to deny them to Chinese. The Court said:[31]

"The fact of this discrimination is admitted. No reason for it is shown, and the conclusion cannot be resisted, that no reason for it exists except hostility to the race and nationality to which the petitioners belong, and which in the eye of the law is not justified. The discrimination is, therefore, illegal. . . ."

In *Truax* v. *Raich,* the right of an individual to have an employer be free in his selection of employees, unrestrained by racial limitations imposed by the State, was held to be protected by the Fourteenth Amendment. Mr. Justice Hughes' opinion of the Court in that case declared[32] that a State's unquestionably, broad police power:

"does not go so far as to make it possible for the State to deny to lawful inhabitants, because of their race or nationality, the ordinary means of earning a livelihood. It requires no argument to show that the right to work for a living in the common occupations of the community is of the very essence of the personal freedom and opportunity that it was the purpose of the Amendment to secure. If this could be refused solely upon the ground of race or nationality, the prohibition of the denial to any person of the equal protection of the laws would be a barren form of words."

Similarly, in *Yu Cong Eng.* v. *Trinidad,*[33] a statutory provision which forbade books of account from being kept in the Chinese language, and thus had the effect of preventing many Chinese merchants from remaining in business, was regarded as a denial of the equal protection and due process safeguards incorporated in the Philippine Autonomy Act.[34]

The Right to Acquire, Use, and Dispose of Property, Without Discrimination Because of Race or Color

There is a line of cases which constitute direct precedent for the proposition that the right to acquire, use, and dispose of property is a right which neither the States nor the Federal Government can abridge or limit on the basis of race or color. The first of these cases is *Buchanan* v. *Warley*,[85] decided thirty years ago by a unanimous Court after extensive deliberation.[36] In that case, a municipal ordinance of the City of Louisville, Kentucky, enacted for the avowed purpose of preventing ill-feeling and conflict between the white and colored races, prohibited any colored person from moving into and occupying as a residence any house in a city block where the majority of dwellings were occupied by white persons. The converse was also prohibited, namely, the establishment of a residence by a white person in a city block where the majority of houses were occupied as residents by Negroes.

Suit was brought by a white property owner against a Negro purchaser to compel specific performance of a contract for the sale of property located in a block where a majority of the residences were occupied by white people. The vendee, by way of answer, asserted that he could not take occupancy of the property under the local ordinance.[37] Reversing the judgment of the Court of Appeals of Kentucky, this Court held the ordinance invalid as a deprivation of the owner's property rights without due process of law.

"Property," the Court stated, "is more than the mere thing which a person owns. It is elementary that it includes the right to acquire, use, and dispose of it. The Constitution protects these essential attributes of property. . . . True it is that dominion over property springing from ownership is not absolute and unqualified. The disposition and use of property may be controlled in the exercise of the police power in the

interest of the public health, convenience, or welfare."[38] How
ever, to impose such a restrain on alienation and acquisition,
based solely on the color of the occupant, was held "not a
legitimate exercise of the police power of the State, and is
in direct violation of the fundamental law enacted in the Fourteenth Amendment of the Constitution preventing state interference with property rights except by due process of law."[39]

In thus holding that the police power of a State—broad as
it is in justifying restrictions upon property rights[40]—cannot
sustain restrictions based solely on color, the Court relied
in no small measure on the rights of colored purchasers to
acquire property, and to use and enjoy it, without being discriminated against because of their color. The Court stated:[41]

"Colored persons are citizens of the United States and have
the right to purchase property and enjoy and use the same
without laws discriminating against them solely on account
of color.[42] These enactments did not deal with the social
rights of men, but with those fundamental rights in property
which it was intended to secure upon the same terms to citizens of every race and color.[43] The Fourteenth Amendment
and these statutes enacted in furtherance of its purpose operate to qualify and entitle a colored man to acquire property
without state legislation discriminating against him solely because of color."

Some of the arguments which are still made, expressly or
tacitly, to support the validity of racial residential segregations
were rejected in *Buchanan* v. *Warley*. The answers given by
the Court then are no less valid today. It was argued that
the ordinance should be upheld because it represented an attempt to deal with the serious and difficult problem of race
hostility. But, answered the Court, the solution of this problem "cannot be promoted by depriving citizens of their constitutional rights and privileges."[44] Similarly, in reply to the
contention that segregation would prevent race conflicts and

promote the public peace, the Court said: "Desirable as this is, and important as is the preservation of the public peace, this aim cannot be accomplished by laws or ordinances which deny rights created or protected by the Federal Constitution." Finally, to the oft-repeated assertion that the property of adjacent owners becomes depreciated when colored persons move into the area, the Court replied: "But property may be acquired by undesirable white neighbors or put to disagreeable though lawful uses with like results."

Although *Harmon* v. *Tyler*,[45] and *City of Richmond* v. *Deans*,[46] were *per curiam* decisions, the factual situations presented in those cases demonstrate the broad basis on which this class of case rests. *Harmon* v. *Tyler* involved a municipal ordinance and a paralleling state statute which, broadly summarized, forbade a Negro person from establishing a residence in a "white community" and a white person from establishing a residence in a "Negro community" except by obtaining the written consent of a majority of the persons of the opposite race living in the community. The suit involved injunctive relief sought by one inhabitant of a "white community" against another owner to restrain him from renting a dwelling to Negro tenants without obtaining the necessary consents. In ruling that the laws did not contravene the provisions of the Fourteenth Amendment and that the relief could not be denied on that ground, the Supreme Court of Louisiana held that the legislation was not discriminatory since it applied equal restraints to both races, that the purpose of the legislation was to discourage social intercourse between the races, and that, unlike *Buchanan* v. *Warley*, there were no restraints on the right to sell or buy property, but only on the right to occupy it as a dwelling. Since the ruling in *Buchanan* v. *Warley* was clearly opposed to each of the grounds relied on by the Louisiana court, it is not surprising that this Court reversed *per curiam* on the authority of that case.

City of Richmond v. *Deans* involved a municipal ordinance which attempted to achieve segregation by prohibiting any person from residing in a city block where the majority of residences were occupied by those with whom such person was forbidden to enter into marriage under state law. The ordinance was thus similar to the one involved in *Buchanan* v. *Warley*. The case, however involved the rights of a Negro purchaser who had entered into a contract to purchase a dwelling in a block where he would have been prohibited from residing under the terms of the ordinance. Upon threats of the ordinance being enforced against him, he filed suit to enjoin the city from doing so. The District Court issued the injunction and the Circuit Court of Appeals, in affirming, ruled that the ordinance, while framed in terms of marriage, was actually based on color alone and, as such, was unconstitutional under *Buchanan* v. *Warley,* and *Harmon* v. *Tyler.* This Court affirmed *per curiam* on the authority of these latter cases.

In summary, therefore, *Buchanan* v. *Warley* and the cases following it have established the broad principle that an individual is protected by the Fifth and Fourteenth Amendments from legislative enactments which limit, solely because of race or color, his right to acquire, use, or dispose of property. As to this right, neither the States nor the Federal Government can impose or enforce general legislative restrictions based exclusively on race or color. Segregation of residential areas on the basis of the race or color of the occupants involves (1) an arbitrary and unreasonable classification which cannot be justified even under the broad police power, and (2) a deprivation without due process of law of the property right of an owner freely to sell, and the correlative right of a buyer freely to purchase and occupy. Persons who are otherwise eligible and willing to acquire property cannot be denied such right simply because they are of a particular race or color. Nor is any such racial or color classification any less unconstitutional because it is made to depend upon the consent of the owners of neighboring property.

In *Fay* v. *New York* this Court in referring to statutes enacted by Congress to implement the Fourteenth Amendment, stated: "For us the majestic generalities of the Fourteenth Amendment are thus reduced to a concrete statutory command when cases involve race or color which is wanting in every other case of alleged discrimination."[47] As we have shown, the respective rights of vendor and purchaser of property to deal with each other freely and without restraint because of each other's race or color are sufficiently clear under the Fourteenth Amendment.[48] Congress, however, has so plainly stated the rights which are secured by that Amendment as to leave no room for doubt in this regard. Section 1978 of the Revised Statutes[49] provides:

"All citizens of the United States shall have the same right, in every State and Territory, as is enjoyed by white citizens thereof to inherit, purchase, lease, sell, hold, and convey real and personal property."[50]

Section 1979 of the Revised Statutes provides:

"Every person who, under color of any statute, ordinance, regulation, custom, or usage, of any State or Territory, subjects, or causes to be subjected, any citizen of the United States or other person within the jurisdiction thereof to the deprivation of any rights, privileges, or immunities secured by the Constitution and laws, shall be liable to the person injured in an action at law, suit in equity, or other proper proceeding for redress."[51]

Section 1978 of the Revised Statutes was derived from Section 1 of the Civil Rights Act of 1866.[52] That statute, which became law while the Fourteenth Amendment was under consideration by Congress, is undoubtedly a clear expression of rights which, if not elsewhere guaranteed by the Constitution, were intended to be secured by the Fourteenth Amendment itself.[53]   The validity of the section, constituting as it does an exercise of the authority given to Congress by Section 6 of the Fourteenth Amendment to enforce its provisions by appropriate legislation, has never been doubted.[54]

In *Virginia* v. *Rives,* speaking of Sections 1977[55] and 1978 of the Revised Statutes, the Court said:

"The plain object of these statutes, as of the Constitution which authorized them, was to place the colored race, in respect of civil rights, upon a level with whites.   They made the rights and responsibilities, civil and criminal, of the two races exactly the same."

Those statutes "partially enumerating what civil rights colored men shall enjoy equally with white persons, founded as they are upon the amendment, are intended for protection against State infringement of those rights."[56]

Again, in *Strauder* v. *West Virginia,* the Court stated that those sections "partially enumerate the rights and immunities intended to be guaranteed by the Constitution . . ."

It was further stated: "This act puts in the form of a statute what had been substantially ordained by the constitutional amendment.   It was a step towards enforcing the constitutional. provisions."

When a State, through its judiciary, enforces a restrictive covenant against a colored citizen of the United States, it thereby denies him the right to purchase or lease property solely on racial grounds.   As regards the particular property involved, it enforces a disability against Negro citizens which does not exist for white citizens.   It creates differences in rights between citizens on the basis of color where Congress has ordained that they shall be "exactly the same."

It is clear, therefore, that the right to acquire, use, and dispose of property is a right which the Constitution protects against governmental restrictions based solely on race or color. There can be no doubt that racial restrictive covenants do impinge upon that right. We submit that judicial enforcement of such covenants interferes also with other constitutional rights, namely, (1) the right to equality of opportunity, without hindrance because of race or color, in securing decent and adequate housing facilities, and (2) the right to equal treatment before the law. *Buchanan* v. *Warley* and the cases following it have settled that no constitutional justification exists for legislative residential segregations based solely on race or color. There remains the question whether judicial decrees enforcing private racial restrictions have any greater constitutional justification. This question is discussed on pages 56-61.

The Right to Compete on Terms of Equality, Without Hindrance Because of Race or Color, in Securing Decent and Adequate Living Accommodations

Truax v. *Raich*[57] holds that the Constitution forbids racial discriminations with respect to "the right to work for a living in the common occupations of the community," because that right "is of the very essence of the personal freedom and opportunity that it was the purpose of the [Fourteenth] Amendment to secure." What is involved in the cases now before the Court is essentially the right to compete on terms of equality, without hindrance because of race or color, in securing decent and adequate living accommodations . The State can no more participate in a denial to its citizens of that right than it can, as *Truax* v. *Raich* holds it cannot, in a denial of the right of equality of opportunity in pursuing "the ordinary means of

earning a livelihood." Both rights are essential attributes of
the "freedom and opportunity" secured by the Constitution.
Neither can be denied on grounds of race or color without
doing violence to our fundamental law.

We need not labor the point. "Housing is a necessary of
life."[58] The right to work for a living is meaningless without
the right to live in a habitable place. It is not suggested that
the Constitution guarantees every man a house of his own
choosing, any more than it guarantees him a job of his own
choosing. What it does guarantee is that the States and the
Federal Government will not exert their authority so as to
deny him equality of opportunity, simply because of his race
or color, in obtaining a job or a house from an employer or
property-owner who would otherwise be able and willing to
give him a job or to sell or rent a house to him.

The Right to Equal Treatment Before the Law

The fundamental principle that all men, regardless of their
race or color, stand equal before the law is imbedded in the
Constitution and laws of the United States. In *Truax* v. *Corrigan* this Court said:

" 'All men are equal before the law,' 'This is a government
of laws and not of men,' 'No man is above the law,' are all
maxims showing the spirit in which legislatures, executives and
courts are expected to make, execute, and apply laws."[59]

The doctrine upholding the equality of all men was given
expression in the Declaration of Independence: "We hold these
truths to be self-evident, that all men are created equal, that
they are endowed by their Creator with certain unalienable
Rights, that among these are Life, Liberty, and the pursuit of
Happiness."

This is more than an abstract pledge. It is given meaning
and effect by the provision of the Fourteenth Amendment that

no person shall be denied the equal protection of the laws. In *Hill* v. *Texas*,[60] Mr. Chief Justice Stone's opinion for the Court stated: "Equal protection of the laws is something more than an abstract right. It is a command which the State must respect, the benefits of which every person may demand."

In *Strauder* v. *West Virginia*,[61] this Court paraphrased the Fourteenth Amendment in these terms:

"What is this but declaring that the law in the States shall be the same for the black as for the white; that *all persons, whether colored or white, shall stand equal before the laws of the States,* and, in regard to the colored race, for whose protection the amendment was primarily designed, that no discrimination shall be made against them by law because of their color?" [Italics added.]

Pursuant to its authority under the Fourteenth Amendment, Congress in 1870 enacted the following statute[62]:

"All persons within the jurisdiction of the United States shall have the same right in every State and Territory in the United States to make and enforce contracts, to sue, be parties, give evidence, and *to the full and equal benefit of all laws and proceedings for the security of person and property as is enjoyed by white citizens,* and shall be subject to like punishment, pains, penalities, taxes, licenses, and exactions of every kind, and none other . . ." [Italics added]

However vague its boundaries, the right to equal treatment before the law certainly requires, as a minimum, that courts shall not establish a rule of law which, in its very terms, makes race or color a controlling factor in its application. *Snowden* v. *Hughes*[63] makes it clear that where a statute or rule of law, fair on its face, is applied differently to those who are entitled to be treated alike, there "is not a denial of equal protection unless there is shown to be present in it an element of intentional or purposeful discrimination."[64].

Judicial enforcement of racial restrictive covenants is quite different. In the first place, the rule of law under which such covenants are enforced is on its face unfair and discriminatory. If the courts which enforce such covenants were merely applying a general rule that all restraints on alienation are enforceable, that might be one thing. It is quite another when the courts do not enforce all restraints on alienation, but do approve those which are based on race and color. We urge that, by force of the Fifth and Fourteenth Amendments and the statutes enacted thereunder, the States and the Federal Government cannot establish rules of law which in their very terms make race or color relevant in their application.

Secondly, even if the rule of law here involved is not discriminatory on its face, there can be no doubt, as has already been shown, that it is applied so as to discriminate against particular minority groups. It has been said that these covenants are enforced against all persons, regardless of their race or color. But the short answer is that, as a practical matter, such covenants are never directed against any but members of particular minority groups.

Judicially-Enforced Racial Restrictions Have No Greater Constitutional Justifications_ Than Legislatively-Imposed Residential Segregations

As has been shown, racial restrictive covenants came to be widely used only after this Court had ruled that racial residential segregation could not be imposed by state or municipal legislatures. They seem to have been adopted as a substitute for such legislation, and have, indeed, well fulfilled that role. Racial restrictive covenants have become so pervasive in this country that the consequences of their enforcement are hardly distinguishable from, and certainly no less serious than, the legislatively-imposed segregations invalidated in Buchanan v. Warley and the cases following it.

The sociological data already set forth show that boundaries beyond which Negroes cannot make their homes are no less real when imposed by restrictive covenants than when imposed by legislation. The result of the constantly increasing use of restrictive covenants has been large-scale compulsory segregation of racial groups with respect to housing. That segregation is not confined to Lousiville, Kentucky, as it was in *Buchanan* v. *Warley;* it has become a national problem; the effects of such covenants are apparent in most of the major urban communities of our country.

Practically and realistically, judicially-enforced racial restrictice covenants have a scope and effect at least as broad as racially restrictive housing legislation. Legally, we submit, they are equally invalid. The Court is not here concerned with the effect or validity of isolated racial restrictive covenants. It is confronted by the existence of such a mass of covenants in different sections of the country as to warrant the assertion that private owners have, by contract, put into effect what amounts to legislation affecting large areas of land—legislation which, if enacted by Congress, by a state legislature, or by a municipal council, would be invalid. Judicial enforcement of racial restrictive covenants has made this a Nation of racial patch quilts, thus presenting constitutional issues which must be resolved by weighing the interests of more than a single vendor or a single vendee. It is the presence of a public interest—the interest of millions of Negroes, Jews, Mexicans, Indians and others who desire to acquire property without restriction because of race or creed, as well as the interest of the non-minority public in removing and avoiding the deleterious social results of segregation—which must invalidate judicial decrees enforcing racial restrictive covenants.

As this Court, speaking through Mr. Justice Holmes, stated:[65]

"Plainly circumstances may so change in time or so differ in space as to clothe with such an interest [i. e., a public interest] what at other times or in other places would be a matter of purely private concern . . . They dispel the notion that what in its immediate aspect may be only a private transaction may not be raised by its class or character to a public affair."

The same point can perhaps be made by paraphrasing the "governing constitutional principle" which this Court has distilled from its decisions under the Contract Clause: When a widely diffused public interest has become enmeshed in a network of multitudinous private arrangements and governmental machinery has been invoked for the effectuation of such arrangements, that public interest cannot be submerged by abstracting one such arrangement from its context and treating it as though it were an isolated private covenant immune from the prohibitions of the Fourteenth and Fifth Amendments.[66]

Marsh v. *Alabama* illustrates the controlling effect of such a public interest in the resolution of issues as to the validity of governmental action under the Due Process Clauses. In that case, the appellant, a Jehovah's Witness, undertook to distribute religious literature on the sidewalk of a town all of the property in which was owned by a single corporation. Although warned that the sidewalk was private property and that distribution of her literature was forbidden, the appellant refused to desist. She was arrested and convicted of violating a state statute making it criminal to enter or remain on the premises of another after having been warned not to do so. In this Court, the appellant contended that her conviction violated her constitutional rights.

In agreeing with the appellant, this Court gave short shrift to the State's contention that the corporation's right to control activities in the company town was "coextensive with the right of a homeowner to regulate the conduct of his guests."[68] It refused, in balancing the property rights of a landowner as against the civil rights of a religious propagandist, to attach the same weight to the right of a corporation to use the state machinery to deny a distributor of religious literature access to an area which, in every respect but ownership, was indistinguishable from any other town or village, as would attach to the right of an individual to invoke governmental organs in order to keep religious solicitors off his parcel of land.[69] It did so because there was another interest which weighed in the balance—the interest of the public, in that case, those inhabitants of the company town who, just as residents of municipalities, had "an identical interest in the functioning of the community in such manner that the channels of communication remain free."[70]

It is of crucial importance, therefore, that those who enter into racial restrictive covenants and who seek to employ the machinery of government in their enforcement "are not acting in matters of merely private concern like the directors or agents of business corporations . They are acting in matters of high public interest,"[71] in that they are attempting to use the power of the State to deny to millions of other persons, solely on racial grounds, the right to decent and adequate housing. To such an attempt at discrimination, the States and the Federal Government cannot proffer the aid and support of their courts.

In *Buchanan* v. *Warley*,[72] the "authority of the State to pass laws in the exercise of the police power, having for their object the promotion of the public health, safety and welfare" was invoked.[73] It was urged that the ordinance should be sustained because it would "promote the public peace by preventing race conflicts."[74] and because "acquisitions by colored persons depreciate property owned in the neighborhood by white persons."[75] While recognizing that the police power of a state is "very broad" and that its exercise "is not to be interfered with by the courts where it is within the scope of legislative authority and the means adopted reasonably tend to accomplish a lawful purpose," the Court held that "it is equally well established that the police power, broad as it is, cannot justify the passage of a law or ordinance which runs counter to the limitations of the Federal Constitution" on the power of government to deny "those fundamental rights in property which it was intended to secure upon the same terms to citizens of every race and color."[76]

Much less may these "fundamental rights" be denied by judicial action at the instance of those who, rather than invoking the broad police power of a State, must rely solely on their interest as neighbors to justify a discrimination which a sovereign State, through its legislature, is without power to impose. As has been noted, the legislative power denied in *Buchanan* v. *Warley* encompassed the interest of white persons in avoiding the depreciation of their property allegedly flowing from the acquisition by colored persons of neighboring property. There can be no doubt of the insufficiency of that interest alone when it, together with the general police powers of the state, was held to be inadequate constitutional justification for racial segregation.

It has been pointed out that racial restrictive covenants came into general use as a substitute for invalidated racial segregation legislation. But, in some respects, the covenant device has been more than a substitute for legislation; it has met the requirements of those desiring to exclude Negroes and other minorities and it has made it possible to do so more certainly and expeditiously. Thus the evils attendant upon racial segregation have been aggravated.

By using the restrictive covenant device, those desirous of imposing racial restrictions can bypass the democratic processes of legislation through which the desirability of such restrictions is passed upon by the elected representatives of the people. Numerous, though relatively small, groups of property owners can, through the covenant device, deny to large groups of people thought to be racially undesirable the right to buy, lease, or use property for long periods of time, indeed often forever. In so doing, they are not required to, nor do they generally, give any consideration to the broader social and economic consequences of their action. Legislative racial segregation can at least be planned so that accommodations can be made for changes in populations, needs, etc. But racial segregation through the covenant device is wholly haphazard. It is subjected to none of the restraining influences on stark racial prejudice which might make for deliberate, considered judgment.

The absence of such a judgment as a possible reasoned basis for the governmental action here involved underlines the views this Court has already announced with respect to the lower degree of deference due to state judicial action as contrasted with legislative action. Here, as in *Bridges* v. *California,*[77] the judgments below "do not come to us encased in the armor wrought by prior legislative deliberation." A legislative "declaration of the State's policy would weigh heavily in any challenge of the law as infringing constitutional limitations."[78] But not so when "the judgment is based on a common law concept of the most general and undefined nature."[79]

*The Decrees Below Cannot Be Justified on Any Theory of
"Waiver" of Constitutional Rights*

It may possibly be contended that, even if judicial enforcement of private racial discriminations violates rights secured
by the Constitution and laws of the United States, the decrees
below are nevertheless valid because they merely enforce agreements of a voluntary nature, and the persons against whom
the decrees are directed cannot be heard to complain because
they have "consented" to such agreements, either actually or
constructively.

We submit that such a contention would be wholly without merit. Whatever its validity as against the white sellers,
the argument could have no application whatsoever against
the colored purchasers. Such persons have obviously relin-
quished none of their constitutional rights merely by entering
into agreements for the purchase and occupancy of property.
These purchasers can hardly be regarded as "parties" to the
restrictive agreements expressly directed against them.

That the property which they agreed to purchase was
already subject to a restrictive covenant is relevant only in so
far as such covenant limited, under state law, the scope of the
seller's rights of alienation. But it begs the question to
conclude that, because the seller under state law cannot legally
sell to him, the colored purchaser is therefore precluded from
asserting that such state law violates *his* constitutional rights.

Moreover, the question of "waiver" involves essentially the
same balancing of public and private interests as that which
is involved in the broader question of constitutional validity.
On the one hand, the State undoubtedly has an interest in
enforcing private contractual arrangements. Persons who
enter into such arrangements ordinarily have a right to rely
upon the aid of the law in their effectuation. But, on the other
hand, there is a countervailing interest against the use of such

aid where it is invoked to enforce a denial of constitutional rights. A white owner of covenanted land may, in a sense, perhaps be regarded as having "waived" his property right of free alienation to the extent of the restriction imposed by the covenant. But the interest of the State in holding him to such a "waiver" is, we submit, clearly outweighed by the interest—protected by the Constitution and laws of the United States—in enabling prospective purchasers to compete on terms of equality, without being discriminated against by governmental action based solely on race or color.

The Case of Corrigan vs. Buckley

Corrigan v. *Buckley*[80] does not foreclose the argument here presented. To be sure, the facts in the *Corrigan* case are essentially similar to those in the present cases. But a careful examination of the Courts ruling discloses that the points now being raised were not settled by that case.

The facts in the *Corrigan* case are simple. In 1921, thirty white owners of property situated in the same block in Washington, D. C., including the plaintiff Buckley and the defendant Corrigan, entered into an agreement that no part of their properties would ever be used or occupied by, or sold or leased or given to, any Negro. In 1922 Corrigan, notwithstanding this restrictive covenant, agreed to sell her lot to the defendant Curtis, a Negro. Buckley thereupon brought suit to enforce the restrictive covenant by enjoining the defendants from executing the contract of sale, and by enjoining Curtis from taking title to the property, and from using or occupying it. The defendants moved to dismiss the bill on the ground that the covenant was "void" in that it was contrary to the Constitution and laws of the United States, and was against public policy. No other issue was presented by the pleadings or the arguments in the lower courts

The defendants' motions were overruled, a final decree of injunction was granted, and was affirmed on appeal by the Court of Appeals for the District of Columbia.[81] The defendants then prayed an appeal to this Court on the ground that such an appeal was authorized under the provisions of Section 250 of the Judicial Code, as it then stood, in that the case was one "involving the construction or application of the Constitution of the United States," and "in which the construction of" certain laws of the United States, namely Sections 1977, 1978, 1979 of the Revised Statutes, were "drawn in question" by the defendants.

This Court held that the appeal should be dismissed for want of jurisdiction. The Court found that, under the pleadings, the only constitutional question involved was that arising from the allegations in the defendants' motions to dismiss, namely, that the covenant which was the basis of the suit was "void" in that it was contrary to and forbidden by the Fifth, Thirteenth, and Fourteenth Amendments. This question was found to be so insubstantial as not to authorize an appeal. The Court reaffirmed its earlier holdings that these Amendments have reference only to governmental action and not to any action of private individuals.[82]

Similarly, the Court held that there was no substantial question as to the "construction" of Sections 1977, 1978 and 1979 of the Revised Statutes. These provisions, like the constitutional amendments under whose sanction they were enacted, "do not in any manner prohibit or invalidate contracts entered into by private individuals in respect to the control and disposition of their own property."[83] The Court also held that the contentions "earnestly pressed by the defendants in this court that the indenture is not only void because contrary to public policy, but is also of such a discriminatory character that a court of equity will not lend its aid by enforcing the specific performance of the covenant" were questions involving consideration of rules not expressed in any constitutional or statutory provision, and therefore could not be reviewed on appeal unless jurisdiction was otherwise acquired.

The appellants had argued before this Court that the decrees of the courts below constituted a violation of the Fifth and Fourteenth Amendments of the Constitution, in that they involved a deprivation of liberty and property without due process of law. Citing *Buchanan* v. *Warley*,[84] and other cases, appellants had urged that the "decrees have all the force of a statute," and that since it would have been beyond the legislative power to authorize enforcement of such covenants, they could not constitutionally be enforced through judicial action. This contention, it may be conceded, is substantially similar to that which petitioners are here pressing. But it is far from clear that this contention was in any way passed upon by this Court in the *Corrigan* case. The only paragraph in the Court's opinion dealing with this contention[85] reads as follows:

"And, while it was further urged in this Court that the decrees of the courts below in themselves deprived the defendants of their liberty and property without due process of law, in violation of the Fifth and Fourteenth Amendments, this contention likewise cannot serve as a jurisdictional basis for the appeal. Assuming that such a contention, if of a substantial character, might have constituted ground for an appeal under paragraph 3 of the Code provision, it was not raised by the petition for the appeal or by any assignment of error, either in the Court of Appeals or in this Court; and it likewise is lacking in substance. The defendants were given a full hearing in both courts; they were not denied any constitutional or statutory right; and there is no semblance of

ground for any contention that the decrees were so plainly
arbitrary and contrary to law as to be acts of mere spoliation.
See *Delmar Jockey Club* v. *Missouri, supra,* 335. Mere error
of a court, if any there be, in a judgment entered after a full
hearing, does not constitute a denial of due process of law.
Central Land Co. v. *Laidley,* 159 U. S. 103, 112; *Jones* v.
Buffalo Creek Coal Co., 245 U. S. 328, 329."

Several observations may be made concerning this paragraph. First, the assertion that the contention "likewise is
lacking in substance" is either dictum or, at most, an alternative holding. Secondly, the reasons which the Court gives
for finding the contention insubstantial make it highly doubtful whether the Court understood the appellants' contention
and was addressing itself to that contention. The appellants
had argued that judicial enforcement was constitutionally equivalent to a legislative enactment. If the Court wished to dispose of that contention, it could hardly have chosen words
less apt. The Court referred merely to the fact that the defendants had been given a full hearing, that they were not
denied any constitutional or statutory right, and that it could
not be said that the decrees were "so plainly arbitrary and
contrary to law as to be acts of mere spoliation." The Court
also referred to the principle, not questioned by the appellants, that due process of law is not denied merely because
a court makes an error of law. If the Court had been of the
view that judicial enforcement of a private contract was not
governmental action within the scope of the Constitution,
that judicial enforcement did not convert the individual action
of the private contracting parties into governmental action,
there surely would have been some indication to that effect
in the Court's opinion. The conclusion is almost inescapable,
therefore, that the Court did not deal with or in any way
pass upon the contention which the appellants had made as

to the constitutional validity of judicial enforcement. We submit, therefore, that the question has not been foreclosed by *Corrigan* v. *Buckley*. Surely this Court will not regard itself as bound, in deciding issues of such constitutional importance as these, by a "precedent" so cloudy and dubious.

IV: PUBLIC POLICY CONSIDERATIONS

Enforcement of racial restrictive covenants is contrary to the public policy of the United States.

Whatever doubts may exist as to the scope of the ruling in *Corrigan* v. *Buckley*,[1] there is no doubt that it leaves wholly open the question whether considerations of public policy bar the judicial enforcement of racial restrictive covenants.[2] We urge upon this Court that the enforcement of such covenants is inconsistent with the public policy of the United States and that upon this independent ground, the judgments in these cases cannot be permitted to stand. Since the public policy upon which we rely is derived from the Federal "Constitution and the laws, and the course of administration and decision"[3], that public policy should be controlling on state courts as well as those of the District of Columbia.[4]

"Public policy is to be ascertained by reference to the laws and legal precedents".[5] Among these are the Fifth and Fourteenth Amendments, the legislation enacted by Congress thereunder, and the decisions of this Court construing and applying such provisions. They may be summarized as establishing most clearly that it is the policy of the United States to deny the sanction of law to racial discriminations, to ensure equality under the law to all persons, irrespective of race, creed or color and, more paricularly, to guarantee to Negroes rights, including the right to use, acquire, and dispose of property, which are in every way equivalent to such rights which are accorded to white persons.

Statutes

In addition to those provisions of the Civil Right Acts having particularly to do with equal property rights, the Civil War marked the beginnings of a series of Acts of Congress through which runs, to this day, a persistent thread of hostility to racial discriminations. Equality of opportunity with white citizens "to make and enforce contracts, to sue, be parties, give evidence, and to the full and equal benefit of all laws and proceedings for the security of persons and property" was required at an early date after emancipation.[6] The same enactment provided that persons other than white citizens "shall be subject to like punishment, pains, penalties, taxes, licenses, and exactions of every kind, and to no other." In the administration of the homestead laws, discrimination on account of race or color was forbidden,[7] and in 1870, the right to vote "without distinction of race, color, or previous condition of servitude" was generally guaranteed.[8] Racial factors were made irrelevant in determining upon qualifications for jury service by the Act of March 1, 1875.[9] And it is of particular significance that Congress has been held to have subjected to criminal penalties persons who conspire to deny to Negroes the right to lease and cultivate lands.[10]

Those charged with the administration of Federal public works, relief, and employment have consistently been enjoined against racial discriminations,[11] and legislation enacted during World War II has included comparable restraints.[12]

Executive Pronouncements

The parallel between the right of employment and the right to decent and adequate housing has already been pointed out. In the light of this close relationship, the Executive Order of President Franklin D. Roosevelt, establishing a Committee on Fair Employment Practice, has particular significance here. In that order,[13] the President said:

"I do hereby reaffirm the policy of the United States that there shall be no discrimination in the employment of workers in defense industries or government because of race, creed, color, or national origin, and I do hereby declare that it is the duty of employers and of labor organizations, in furtherance of said policy and of this order, to provide for the full and equitable participation of all workers in defense industries, without discrimination because of race, creed, color, or national origin."

This Governmental policy against racial discrimination in employment has been particularized with respect to civil service[14] and employment by Government contractors and subcontractors.[15]

It is not necessary to rely on the analogy between employment and housing, however, in order to establish a public policy directly relevant here. For both Presidents Roosevelt and Truman have spoken of "the right to a decent home" as part of "a second Bill of Rights",[16] and "of the basic rights which every citizen in a truly democratic society must possess."[17]

International Agreements

The Charter of the United Nations,[18] approved as a treaty by the Senate on July 28, 1945,[19] provides in its preamble, among other things, that:

"We the peoples of the United Nations, determined . . . to reaffirm faith in fundamental human rights, in the dignity and worth of the human person, in the equal rights of men and women . . . and to promote social progress and better standards of life in larger freedom, and for these ends to practice tolerance . . . have resolved to combine our efforts to accomplish these aims."[20]

In Article 55 of the Charter, the United Nations agree to promote "universal respect for, and observance of, human rights and fundamental freedoms for all without distinction as to race, sex, language, or religion."[21]

By Article 56, "All Members pledge themselves to take joint and separate action in co-operation with the Organization for the achievement of the purposes set forth in Article 55."[22]

The United Nations General Assembly, on November 19, 1946, adopted the following resolution:

"The General Assembly declares that it is in the higher interests of Humanity to put an immediate end to religious and so-called racial persecutions and discrimination, and calls on the Governments and responsible authorities to conform both to the letter and to the spirit of the Charter of the United Nations, and to take the most prompt and energetic steps to that end."[23]

At the Inter-American Conference on Problems of War and Peace held at Mexico City in 1945, at which the Act of Chapultepec of March, 1945, was agreed upon, the United States Delegation submitted a draft resolution, which was later adopted by the Conference, entitled "Economic Charter of the Americas." The following statement appears in this resolution:[24]

"The fundamental economic aspiration of the peoples of the Americas, in common with peoples everywhere, is to be able to exercise effectively their natural right to live decently. . . ."[25]

Another resolution adopted by the Conference[26] provides:

"Whereas: World peace cannot be consolidated until men are able to exercise their basic rights without distinction as to race or religion, The Inter-American Conference on Problems of War and Peace resolves:

"1. To reaffirm the principle, recognized by all the American States, of equality of rights and opportunities for all men, regardless of race or religion.

"2. To recommend that the Governments of the American Republics, without jeopardizing freedom of expression, either oral or written, make every effort to prevent in their respective countries all acts which may provoke discrimination among individuals because of race or religion."[27]

At the conclusion of this Conference, the Secretary of State issued a statement in which he said:

". . . in the Declaration of Mexico and in other resolutions, we have rededicated ourselves at this Conference to American principles of humanity and to raising the standards of living of our peoples, so that all men and women in these republics may live decently in peace, in liberty, and in security. That is the ultimate objective of the program for social and economic co-operation which has been agreed upon at Mexico City."[28]

A particularly pertinent statement, also in the form of a Resolution, was made at and adopted by The Eighth International Conference of American States at Lima, Peru, in 1938. This Resolution, approved by the Conference on December 23, 1938, reads:

"The Republics represented at the Eighth International Conference of American States declare:

"1. That, in accordance with the fundamental principle of equality before the Law, any persecution on account of racial or religious motives which makes it impossible for a group of human beings to live decently, is contrary to the political and juridical systems of America.

"2. That the democratic conception of the State guarantees to all individuals the conditions essential for carrying on their legitimate activities with self-respect.

"3. That they will always apply these principles of human solidarity."[29]

Conclusion

In refusing to enforce a contract on grounds of public policy, this Court, in an opinion by Mr. Justice Holmes, said: "To compel the specific performance of contracts still is the exception, not the rule, and courts would be slow to compel it in cases where it appears that paramount interests will or even may be interfered with by their action . . . if it appears that an injunction would be against public policy, the court properly may refuse to be made an instrument for such a result".[30]

The legislative, executive, and international pronouncements set out above reflect a public policy wholly inconsistent with the enforcement of racial restrictive covenants. The public interest in racial segregation is at least as great as public interest in whether a railroad station should be built in a certain place, the question involved in the *Beasley* case. There, as here, an attempt to limit the use to which land could be put by means of a restrictive covenant was involved. And the Court there, as we think it should here, refused the injunction sought, noting some reluctance in any event specifically to enforce such restraints, but resting on the paramount interests of the public as a controlling reason for denying equitable relief.

A public policy against enforcement of racial restrictive covenants is the ground upon which the High Order of Ontario has denied equitable relief in a recent decision.[31] After referring to similar principles of political conduct, the court said:

"The consequences of judicial approbation of such a covenant are portentous. If sale of a piece of land can be prohibited to Jews, it can equally be prohibited to Protestants, Catholics or other groups or denominations. If the sale of one piece of land can be so prohibited, the sale of other pieces of land can likewise be prohibited. In my opinion, nothing could be more calculated to create or deepen divisions between existing religious and ethnic groups in this Province, or in this country, than the sanction of a method of land transfer which would permit the segregation and confinement of particular groups to particular business or residential areas, or conversely, would exclude particular groups from particular business or residential areas."

The court then went on to note "the unlikelihood of such a policy as a legislative measure". In this country, we need not speculate about likelihoods; such a legislative measure would be unconstitutional. For that reason, we submit that even if the decrees below are not stricken on specific constitutional grounds, they may properly be set aside as being inconsistent with the public policy of the United States.

V: RESTRAINTS ON ALIENATION

Enforcement of racial restrictive covenants contravenes settled principles governing the validity of restraints on alienation and is inequitable.

Racial covenants constitute invalid restraints on alienation.

In Nos. 290 and 291, the Court of Appeals for the District of Columbia held that racially restrictive covenants do not constitute illegal restraints on alienation in the District of Columbia. We contend, on the contrary, that the common law invalidates the effort to exclude, through restraints on alienation of real property, the members of groups based on race or color.

Local Decisions

It was not until *Hundley* v. *Gorewitz*,[1] decided in December, 1942, that the Court of Appeals of the District of Columbia for the first time noted the argument that "the covenant constitutes an undue and unlawful restraint on alienation." The issue was not discussed at that time, the court contenting itself with the statement that "in view of the consistent adjudications in similar cases, it must now be conceded that the settled law in this jurisdiction is that such covenants as this are valid and enforceable in equity by way of injunction".[2] The earlier District covenant cases, which the court cites as conclusive, had not, however, passed upon the alienation issue. The matter was first canvassed on its merits in *Mays* v. *Burgess*,[3] decided in January, 1945, in which the majority of the court held a racially restrictive covenant, limited in time, not to be invalid, because it was not a total restraint.[4] In the instant cases, the court below rests on the opinion in the *Mays* case, and extends its holding to a perpetual restriction. It is clear from this history that the District's view of the effect of the common law rules against restraints upon racial agreements, far from being long established or deeply rooted, is hardly sown.

Common Law Rules Against Restraint on Alienation

Post medieval common law developed a general rule against restraints on the alienation of property owned in fee which has become part of the unwritten law of every Anglo-American jurisdiction. As the Restatement of Property puts it:[5]

"The underlying principle which operates throughout the field of property law is that freedom to alienate property interests which one may own is essential to the welfare of society. The basis for the assumption that social welfare requires freedom of alienation . . . is . . . found to rest in part upon the necessity of maintaining a society controlled primarily by its living members, in part upon the social desirability of facilitating the utilization of wealth, and in part upon the social desirability of keeping property responsive to the current exigencies of its current beneficial owners. Restraints on alienation are from their very nature inconsistent with the policy of freedom of alienation. Thus, to uphold them, justification must be found in the objective that is thereby sought to be accomplished or on the ground that the interference with alienation in the particular case is so negligible that the major policies furthered by freedom of alienation are not materially hampered."[6]

It is fair to say that in the latter part of the last century, and the first two decades of this, the unfolding of this policy of free alienability tended toward the invalidation of substantial restraints on conveyances of real property. A few early British cases,[7] and some isolated state decisions in this country[8] looked the other way, but they felt the great weight of judicial and professional disapproval. The modern cases and the views of the recognized authorities formulated the doctrine of freedom so broadly that one would have been justified in forecasting, in 1915, that conveyors' attempts to forbid consequent transfer to any numerically significant group would be invalidated—if the announced policies supporting the rule against restraints were to control without dilution from different streams of social or political policy. If, for instance, a conveyor had attempted to prohibit future sale of his land to any New Englander, or college graduate, he would properly have been warned that the restraint would probably be invalidated because the excluded class was too large.[9]

It is doubly significant that the only cases in the United States upholding the exclusion of a social group of considerable size are the racial covenant cases, and, that, except for a single case from a non-common law jurisdiction,[10] all these cases were decided after this Court had struck down legislative housing segregation in *Buchanan* v. *Warley*.[11] The considerations which appear to have moved these courts may be gathered from the American Law Institute's treatment of racially restrictive restraints. As Justice Edgerton pointed out below,[12] covenants against Negroes would seem to be marked as unreasonable, and therefore invalid, by the Restatement's stated criteria.[13] Nevertheless, the Institute has a specific provision upholding such restraints, *"in states where the social conditions render desirable the exclusion of the racial or social group involved from the area in question"* (italics supplied), and the Restatements' full comment makes even plainer that the dominant influence is the achievement of racial or social segregation, where that is thought to be desirable, rather than the achievement of the policies historically underlying the rule against restraints.[14]

There are similar indications in various of the cases uphold-

ing racial restraints that the decisive factor has been judicial
approval, or at least acceptance, of a policy of residential segregation as outweighing the requirements of free alienability.
In the *Queensborough* case, the first decision passing upon
racial restrictions, the Louisiana court thought "that it would
be unfortunate, if our system of land tenure were so hide-
bound, or if the public policy of the general government or
of the state where so narrow, as to render impracticable a
scheme such as the one in question in this case, whereby an
owner has sought to dispose of his property advantageously
to himself and beneficially to the city wherein it lies."[15] In
Parmalee v. *Morris*,[16] the court felt that "The law is powerless
to eradicate racial instincts or to abolish distinctions which some
citizens do draw on account of racial differences in relation to
their matter of purely private concern. For the law to attempt
to abolish these distinctions in the private dealings between
individuals would only serve to accentuate the difficulties which
the situation presents."[17] Dean Ribble[18] pithily summarizes
the attitude of the courts which uphold substantial restraints:
"Finally, it may be suggested that a court's finding that the
restraint is reasonable, and consequently valid, is simply a way
of saying that the court believes that the policies favoring the
restraint outweigh the policies opposed to it, so that the state's
welfare is better served by allowing the validity of the restraint than by denying it."[19]

The historical conception of improper restraints on alienation has had sufficient force to compel a number of state courts
to invalidate racial restraints on sales or leases,[20] but these
courts simultaneously uphold restrictions against *use or occupancy* by the excluded group.[21]

"Now it is apparent that, however a restraint upon occupancy may be classified in theory, in practice it is a restraint
upon alienation in this type of case. Negroes and Asiatics,

against whom the restriction is directed, are not likely to buy land which they themselves cannot occupy, and which they cannot even lease to members of their own race. The actual effect of the restriction is to exclude members of these races as potential purchasers of the land. Restraints upon occupancy, nevertheless, have been sustained in almost every case in which the problem has arisen. This state of the authority seems explicable only upon the supposition that the courts have believed the social interest to require the toleration of these restrictions, that they have felt precluded by supposed authority from upholding the restrictions when phrased directly as restraints upon alienation, but have eagerly seized upon the theoretical difference between a restraint upon alienation and a restraint upon occupancy to justify their conclusions.[22] The American Law Institute explicitly recognizes the identity of the two restrictions by providing the same rule for restraints on use by excluded groups as on sales.[23]

In short, the carving out of racial real estate limitations from the application of the common-law rule against restraints on alienation has largely resulted from intervention of sympathy with, or affirmative acceptance of, the social interest in racial residential segregation, rather than from a development of the original policy premises of the common-law doctrines of free alienability. But the Federal courts, including those in the District of Columbia, should, at the very least, refrain from affirmative use of segregation policies in applying and developing the rules of real property or contract law.[24] Thus, in determining whether the exclusion of such a large group as the Negro race constitutes an unlawful restraint, the courts of the District of Colmbia might weigh the fundamental rationale of the common-law rule, its applicability to the present day, and the proper extent of allowable restrictions on alienees, but should be bound to consider the excluded group as if it were composed of an equal number of white, or white and colored, persons.

The racial factor apart, it would seem clear that a restraint which perpetually excluded at least a quarter of the population of the District of Columbia, and some 20,000,000 American citizens,[25] should not be upheld. The owner's freedom to convey would plainly be substantially impaired, and no adequate counterbalancing considerations could exist. The discussion in the pertinent portion of the Restatement of Property,[26] much of which we have quoted, strongly tends toward the invalidation of restraints where "the number of persons to whom alienation is prohibited is large," and only exempts racial or social restrictions because of the presumed special social interest in segregation in certain States. When the "social importance" of the objective sought to be accomplished by the imposition of such a restraint is weighed against the "evils which flow from interfering with the power of alienation" annulment of the restriction is clearly required.[27] The main lines of authority, exclusive of the racial restraint cases, support this view, as the Restatement's codification sufficiently proves.[28]

The many cases upholding nonracial building or use restrictions are not opposed, since in most instances the "curtailment of the power of alienation is so slight that no social danger is involved"[29] and all involve a social value which may properly be encouraged by the courts at the expense of free alienability.[30]

Enforcement of the Covenants Would Be Inequitable

Respondents in Nos 290 and 291 do not show themselves entitled to an injunction merely by proving their covenants valid at common law and enforceable under the Constitution. "An appeal to the equity jurisdiction conferred on federal district courts is an appeal to the sound discretion which guides the determinations of courts of equity."[31]   And courts of equity have traditionally refused their aid, either where "the plaintiff is using the right asserted contrary to the public interest,"[32] or where, all special public interest aside, "issuance of an injunction would subject the defendant to grossly disproportionate hardship."[33]   To enjoin petitioners and require their removal from their homes would breach both of these historic bulwarks which equity has erected against judicial injustice.   As Mr. Justice Frankfurter has stated,[34] "the function of the judiciary is not so limited that it must sanction the use of the federal courts as instruments of injustice in disregard of moral and equitable principles which have been part of the law for centuries."

There is no doubt about the evil effect upon the housing conditions and welfare of Negroes of the systematic and wholesale residential segregation in the District of Columbia which racial covenants have produced.   The sum of the matter is that "Negroes are increasingly being forced into a few overcrowded slums" and "the chief weapon in the effort to keep Negroes from moving out of overcrowded quarters into white neighborhoods is the restrictive covenant."[35]   The prejudice to the general welfare thus created by the cumulative impact of this "network of multitudinous private arrangements" plainly warrants a court of equity in staying its hand and leaving the covenantors to whatever strictly legal remedies they may have.[36]   Application of established equitable doctrines in the field of racial restrictive covenants is hardly novel; courts have long refused injunctions when enforcement has been found to be injurious to the general interests of the covenanting property owners, even though certain individual owners may still desire to retain segregation.[37]

The private harm to these particular colored grantees is also

sufficient to outweigh any benefits which respondents may
feel will accrue to them through continued residential segregation. These grantees purchased their homes only after many
hardships and long-continued efforts to obtain adequate housing; several of the grantees had been evicted from rented
houses by owners seeking personal occupancy. In the District
of Columbia there is undeniably an acute shortage of houses
for Negroes, even at prices inflated beyond those which white
persons would have to pay.[38] If petitioners and other grantees
of the same class are forced to move, they will probably face
grave difficulties in finding adequate housing, one of the true
essentials of life. If they are allowed to remain, respondents
will at most suffer an invasion of the lesser social interest in
privacy or choice of neighbors.

*   *   *

The Court should not hesitate, we believe, to decide these
issues of restraints on alienation and the equitable right to an
injunction. These are no longer local law matters, of peculiar
concern to the District, which should be left to the courts of
the District.[39] The determination of these issues largely turns
upon general social considerations of the greatest importance,
and is intimately related to a federal public policy of which
this Court, and not the District of Columbia courts, is the final
arbiter. Nor are the questions presented for decision unique
to the District, or governable by common-law developments
special to this area; their nation-wide significance is attested by
the geographical distribution of the decisions sustaining racial
covenants, as well as by the related cases now on this Court's
docket.

Moreover, it cannot be said that on either issue the courts
of the District of Columbia are enforcing a well-established
rule, or one adopted after careful review. Decision on the
application of the rule against restraints has come very late

and almost by inadvertence. The propriety of equitable relief appears never to have had full consideration, not even in the instant cases. As the highest court in the judicial system of the District, this Court should exercise its power to determine the controlling law for the nation's capital.[40]

VI: CONCLUSION

Statutory residential segregation based on race or color does not exist in this country because the Supreme Court struck it down as violative of the Constitution. Actual segregation, rooted in ignorance, bigotry and prejudice, and nurtured by the opportunities it affords for monetary gains from the supposed beneficiaries and real victims alike, does exist because private racial restrictions are enforced by courts. These covenants are injurious to our order and productive of growing antagonisms destructive of the integrity of our society. Inadequate shelter, disease, juvenile delinquency are some of the major evils directly traceable to racial restrictive covenants. Restraints on alienation of real property are generally regarded as contrary to the policy of the States; yet restrictive racial covenants have been upheld by State courts, some on the tenuous ground that a restriction against use or occupancy is somehow, in the eyes of the law, entitled to Constitutional approval although a restriction against ownership alone is condemned. There is no basis for such a distinction. The covenant restricting use and occupation works precisely the same evils as the covenant against ownership by the members of the proscribed race or color.

The areas controlled by restrictive racial covenants are rapidly expanding in urban centers, and the resulting danger to our free institutions is imminent. Courts judge the validity of statutes not merely by what is done under them but by what may be done under them. The same rule must be applied to these covenants in which the public interest has become enmeshed. Restricted areas could be expanded through covenants until whole groups of citizens, selected by race or color or creed or ancestry, could be exiled from this nation forever. Supposed freedom of contract may not be used to further such ends. This Court has pointed out that the Constitution does not speak of freedom of contract. "It speaks of liberty and prohibits the deprivation of liberty without due process of law."[1]

Race hostilities will not disappear when and if this Court determines that racial restrictive covenants are abhorrent to the law of the land. Neither will a measure of segregation, existing through the voluntary choice of the people concerned. But, as this Court said in *Buchanan* v. *Warley*,[2] the solution of the problem of race hostility "cannot be promoted by depriving citizens of their constitutional rights and privileges."

GENERAL BIBLIOGRAPHY

MISCELLANEOUS BOOKS

An American Dilemma. By Gunnar Myrdal, 1944.
Patterns of Negro Segregation. By Charles S. Johnson, 1943.
The Negro's Share. By Richard Sterner, 1943.
The Legal Status of the Negro. By Charles S. Mangum, 1940.
Black Metropolis. By St. Clair Drake and H. R. Clayton, 1945.
Negro Problems in Cities. By T. J. Woofter, 1928.
The Housing of Negroes in Washington. By W. H. Jones, 1929.
Hemmed In. By Robert C. Weaver.

LEGAL BOOKS

Adoption of the Fourteenth Amendment. By Horace Flack, 1908.
Restraints Upon the Alienation of Property. By John C. Gray, 1895.
The Law of Future Interests. By Lewis M. Simes, 1936.
Real Covenants and Other Interests Which "Run With Land." By Charles
   E. Clark, 1947.
Modern Law of Real Property. By Geoffrey Cheshire, 4th. ed., 1937.

REPORTS

Report of the President's Committee on Civil Rights, 1947.
Report on Negro Housing of the President's Conference on Home Building
   and Home Ownership, 1932.
Report on Housing and Juvenile Delinquency, National Conference on
   Prevention and Control of Juvenile Delinquency, 1946.
Report of the Chicago Housing Authority for the Fiscal Year Ending June 30,
   1947.
Report of Pennsylvania State Temporary Commission on the Condition of
   the Urban Colored Population, 1943.

REFERENCES

I: RACIAL RESTRICTIVE COVENANTS

[1] The only case decided prior to 1915 was Gandolfo v. Hartman, 49 Fed. 181 (C.C.S.C. Cal.), decided in 1892, involving a restriction against Chinese.

[2] 245 U.S. 60.

[3] See infra, pp. 19-21; *An American Dilemma*, by Gunnar Myrdal, 1944, pp. 622-627; *Patterns of Negro Segregation*, by Charles S. Johnson, 1943, pp. 172-176; *The Negro's Share*, by Richard Sterner, 1943, pp. 205-209; *The Legal Status of the Negro*, by Charles S. Mangrum, 1940, pp. 140-152.

[4] See infra, pp. 19-21.

[5] See infra, p. 21 and pp. 78-80.

[6] Nos. 290-291, R. 380.

[7] No. 87, R. 13, 16, 37, 39, 42, 60.

[8] No. 72, R. 154-155.

[9] As in Nos. 290-291 (R. 380-382).

[10] As in Nos. 72 and 87.

[11] *The American Dilemma*, by Gunner Myrdal p. 376; cf. pp. 1290-1292; cf. *The Negro's Share*, by Richard Sterner, 1943, p. 190.

[12] The above tables are taken from "Validity of Anti-Negro Restrictive Covenants: A Reconsideration of the Problem," by Kahen (12 *University of Chicago Law Review*, 198, 202). They are based upon U.S. Census data for 1910, 1920, 1930, and 1940, and illustrate the extent to which Negroes have flocked to the cities in the last three decades.

[13] See *An American Dilemma*, by Gunnar Myrdal, 1944, pp. 618-627, and pp. 1125-1128 (Appendix 7: "Distribution of Negro Residences in Selected Cities"); *Black Metropolis*, by St. Clair Drake and H. R. Cayton, 1945, chapter 8, especially pp. 175-178.

[14] In Nos. 290-291, 162 F. 2d, at 243-245, and in Mays v. Burgess, 147 F. 2d 869, at 876-878.

[15] Report on Negro Housing (1932), pp. 45, 46.

[16] Negro housing conditions and segregation in the District of Columbia are described in Justice Edgerton's opinion below in Nos. 290 and 291, and in Mays v. Burgess, 147 F. 2d 869, 152 F. 2d 123; in the Report of the President's Committee on Civil Rights, pp. 91-92; in "Negro Housing— Capital Sets Record for U. S. in Unalleviated Wretchedness of Slums", by Agnes E. Meyer, the *Washington Post*, Feb. 6, 1944; and in "The Nation's Capital", by Lohman and Embree, 36 *Survey Graphic*, No. 1 (Jan., 1947), 33,

88   *Prejudice and Property*

35, 37. These sources prove that the drastic scarcity of housing in the District is universally recognized, and that the housing position of Negroes is particularly acute.

[17] *Negro Problems in Cities,* by T. J. Woofter, 1928, pp. 121-135; *An American Dilemma,* by Gunnar Myrdal, pp. 379, 623, 625; *Black Metropolis,* by St. Clair Drake and H. R. Clayton, 1945, pp. 185-186, 206-207; "Relationship Between Condition of Dwellings and Rentals, by Race," by Robinson, 1946, 22 *Journal of Land and Public Utilities Economics,* 296; Differential Rents for White and Negro Families," by Sherman, 3 *Journal of Housing,* (No. 8, Aug. 1946), 169.

[18] Report on Negro Housing of the President's Conference on Home Building and Home Ownership (1932), pp. 52, 71-72, 145; Report on Housing and Juvenile Delinfuency, National Conference on Prevention and Control of Juvenile Delinquency (called by the Attorney General), 1946, pp. 1-8, 12-13.

[19] *An American Dilemma,* by Gunnar Myrdal, 1944, p. 376; Report on Negro Housing, 1932, pp. 143-198; "The Measurement of Ecological Segregation", by Jahn, Schmid and Schrag, 1947, 12 *American Sociological Review,* 293, 302-303; letter of Surgeon General Parran, quoted herein.

[20] Report of the President's Committee on Civil Rights, 1947, passim, especially pp. 139-148.

[21] See infra, pp. 18-19.

[22] Report of the President's Committee on Civil Rights, 1947, p. 68; "Race Restrictive Housing Covenants," by Weaver, 1944, 20 *Journal of Land and Public Utilities Economics,* 183, 185.

[23] *Black Metropolis,* by St. Clair Drake and H. R. Cayton, 1945, pp. 113, 176-179, 182-190; *An American Dilemma,* by Gunnar Myrdal, 1944, p. 624; *Hemmed In,* by Robert C. Weaver, p. 1; *The Negro's Share,* by Richard Sterner, 1943, pp. 207-208; Report of the Chicago Housing Authority for the fiscal year ending June 30, 1947, pp. 14, 38. It has been estimated that 80% of the residential area of the city is already covered by covenants; and the strategic location of the restricted region around the established Negro zone is clear. According to the American Council on Race Relations, evidence introduced in a recent racial covenant case in Chicago (Tovey v. Levy), based upon a study of the recorded restrictions in approximately two-thirds of the city's area, bears out this conclusion.

[24] "Housing Problems of Minority Groups in Los Angeles", by Spaulding, 248 *Annals of the American Academy of Social and Political Science,* November, 1946, pp. 220-22.

[25] The Association gathered its information at a meeting on Race Restrictive Covenants, held at Chicago, July 9-10, 1945.

[26] Cf. "Housing: Detroit's Time Bomb", by Velie, *Collier's,* Nov. 23, 1946.

[27] "None Other Than Caucasian," by Dean, *Architectural Forum,* Oct. 1947.

[28] Report of the President's Committee, p. 91; cf. Justice Edgerton, dissenting below 162 F. 2d, at 244, and in Mays v. Burgess, 147 F. 2d 869, at 876-877.

[29] *The Housing of Negroes in Washington,* by W. H. Jones, 1929, p. 70.

[30] Supra, pp. 28-29.

[31] Address before the Annual Conference of the National Urban League, at Columbus, Ohio, October 2, 1944.

[32] October 28-November 2, 1946.

[33] *An America Dilemma* by Gunnar Myrdal, 1946, p. 624, cf. p. 527; *The Negro's Share,* by Richard Sterner, 1943, pp. 200-207. Of similar view as to the decisive effect of covenants in maintaining confined zones of segregation are "Race Restrictive Housing Covenants" by Weaver, 1944, 20 *Journal of Land and Public Utilities Economics* 183; "Housing in a Democracy", by Weaver, 244 *Annals of the American Academy of Political and Social Science* 95, March, 1946; "Relationship Between Condition of Dwellings and Rentals, by Race", by Robinson, 1946, 22 *Journal of Land and Public Utilities Economics* 296, pp. 301-302. See also the specific studies of Chicago, New York, and Los Angeles cited above.

[35] Supra, pp. 13-15.

[36] In his dissent in Nos. 290 and 291 below (162 F. 2d, at 244).

[37] Supra, pp. 14-20.

[38] See "The Power of Restrictive Covenants", by Miller, 36 *Survey Graphic,* No. 1, Jan., 1947, 46; Consolidated Brief for Petitioners in Nos. 290-291, pp. 90-92.

[39] See letter of the Administrator of the Housing and Home Finance Agency, quoted herein; Report of the President's Committee on Civil Rights, 1947, p. 68; *The Negro's Share,* by Richard Sterner, 1943, pp. 208-209; "Homes for Aryans Only", by Charles Abrams, 3 *Commentary,* No. 5, May, 1947, p. 421; "Discriminatory Restrictive Covenants—A Challenge to the American Bar", address by Charles Abrams before the Bar Association of the City of New York, Feb. 19, 1947; "Housing Problems of Minority Groups in Los Angeles", by Spaulding, 248 *Annals of the American Academy of Social and Political Science,* Nov., 1946, p. 220; "None Other Than Caucasian", by Dean, *Architectural Forum,* Oct., 1947; "The Use of Deed Restrictions in Subdivision Development", by Monchow, 1928; "Northern Ways", by Weaver, 36 *Survey Graphic,* Jan., 1947, pp. 43, 45; Report of Pennsylvania State Temporary Commission on the Condition of the Urban Colored Population, 1943, p. 131 et. seq.

[40] Report of the President's Committee on Civil Rights, 1947, p. 69.

[41] Most of the cases are collected in "Racial Residential Segregation by State Court Enforcement of Restrictive Agreements, Covenants or Conditions in Deeds is Unconstitutional", by McGovney, 1945, 33 *California Law Review* 5, 6-12.

[42] Buchanan v. Warley, 245 U. S. 60.

[43] Alabama: *Wyatt* v. *Adair,* 215 Ala. 363 (1926).

California: *Los Angeles Inv. Co.* v. *Gary,* 181 Cal. 680 (1919); *Janss Investment Co.* v. *Walden,* 196 Cal. 753 (1925); *Wayt* v. *Patee,* 205 Cal. 46 1928).

Colorado: *Chandler* v. *Ziegler,* 88 Colo. 1 (1930); *Steward* v. *Cronan,* 105 Colo. 393 (1940).

Georgia: *Dooley* v. *Savannah Bank & Trust Co.,* 199 Ga. 353 (1945).

Illinois: *Burke* v. *Kleiman.* 277 Ill. App. 519, 534.

Kansas: *Clark* v. *Vaughan,* 131 Kan. 438 (1930).

Kentucky: *United Cooperative Realty Co.* v. *Hawkins,* 269 Ky. 563 (1937).

Louisiana: *Queensborough Land Co.* v. *Cazeaux,* 136 La. 724 (1915).

Maryland: *Meade v. Dennistone,* 173 Md. 295 (1938); *Scholtes* v. *Mc-Colgan,* 184 Md. 480, 487-488 (1945).

Michigan: *Parmalee* v. *Morris,* 218 Mich. 625 (1922); *Schulte* v. *Starks,* 238 Mich. 102 (1927); Cf. *Porter* v. *Barrett,* 233 Mich. 373 (1925) (invalidating restraint on sale or lease on common-law grounds).

Missouri: *Koehler* v. *Rowland,* 275 Mo. 573 (1918); *Porter* v. *Pryor,* 164 S. W. 2d 353 (Mo. 1942); *Porter* v. *Johnson,* 232 Mo. App. 1150 (1938); *Thornhill* v. *Herdt,* 130 S. W. 2d 175 (Mo. App. 1939).

New Jersey: *Lion's Head Lake* v. *Brzezinski,* 23 N. J. Misc. 290 (1945) (2nd Dist. Ct. of Paterson); But cf. *Miller v. Jersey Coast Resorts Corp.,* 98 N. J. Eq. 289, 297 (Ct. Ch. 1925) (dictum that a restrictive covenant prohibiting Jews from purchasing land would be unconstitutional).

New York: *Ridgway* v. *Cockburn,* 163 Misc. 511 (Sup. Ct. Westchester Co., 1937; *Dury* v. *Neely,* 69 N. Y. Supp. 2d 677 (Sup. Ct. Queens Co., 1942); *Kemp* v. *Rubin,* 188 Misc. 310, 69 N. Y. Supp. 2d 680 (Sup. Ct., Queens Co., 1947).

North Carolina: *Vernon* v. *R. J. Reynolds Realty Co.,* 226 N. C. 58 (1946).

Ohio: *Perkins* v. *Trustees of Monroe Ave. Church,* 79 Ohio App. 457, 70 N. E. 2d 487 (1946), appeal dismissed, 72 N. E. 2d 97 (Ohio, 1947), pending on petition for writ of certiorari, No. 153, this Term.

Oklahoma: *Lyons* v. *Wallen,* 191 Okla. 567 (1942); *Hemsley* v. *Sage,* 194 Okla. 669 (1944); *Hemsley* v. *Hough,* 195 Okla. 298 (1945).

Texas: *Liberty Annex Corp.* v. *Dallas,* 289 S. W. 1067, 1069 (Tex. Civ. App., 1927), affirmed 295 S. W. 591, 592 (Com. of App. 1927).

West Virginia: *White* v. *White,* 108 W. Va. 128, 147 (1929).

Wisconsin: *Doherty* v. *Rice,* 240 Wisc. 389 (1942).

District of Columbia: *Corrigan* v. *Buckley,* 299 Fed. 899 (1924), appeal dismissed, 271 U. S. 323; *Torrey* v. *Wolfes,* 6 F. 2d 702 (1925); *Cornish* v. *O'Donoghue,* 20 F. 2d 983 (1929), certiorari denied, 279 U. S. 871; *Russell* v. *Wallace,* 30 F. 2d 981 (1929), certiorari denied, 279 U. S. 871; *Edwards* v. *West Woodridge Theater Co.,* 55 F. 2d 524, 526 (1931); *Grady* v. *Garland,* 89 F. 2d 817 (1937), certiorari denied, 302 U. S. 694; *Hundley* v. *Gorewitz,* 132 F. 2d 23, 24 (1942); *Mays* v. *Burgess,* 147 F. 2d 869

(1945), certiorari denied, 395 U. S. 868, rehearing denied, 325 U. S. 896.

California, Maryland, Michigan, Ohio, and West Virginia invalidate racial restrictions on sales or lease, on common-law grounds, but uphold similar restrictions on use or occupancy, and in those states racial covenants appear to take the form of restrictions on "use or occupancy" by excluded groups; see *infra*, pp. 75-83 for discussion of this distinction and of the common-law rule on restraints against alienation.

⁴⁴ Gandolfo v. Hartman, 49 Fed. 181, C. C. S. D. California 1892.

⁴⁵ Miller v. Jersey Coast Resorts Corp., 98 New Jersey Equity 289, 297 (Ct. Ch. 1925).

⁴⁶ 271 U. S. 323.

⁴⁷ See, e.g., Lyons v. Walles, 191 Okla. 567, 569; United Cooperative Realty Co. v. Hawkins, 269 Ky. 563; Meade v. Dennistone, 173 Md. 295, 302; Doherty v. Rice, 240 Wisc. 389, 396-397; Chandler v. Ziegler, 88 Colo. 1, 5; Dooley v. Savannah Bank & Trust Co., 199 Ga. 353, 364; Liberty Annex Corp. v. Dallas, 289 S. W. 1067, 1069 (Tex. Civ. App.); Perkins v. Trustees of Monroe Ave. Church, 79 Ohio App. 457, 70 N. E. 2d 487, appeal dismissed, 72 N. E. 2d 97, Ohio, pending on petition for writ of certiorari, No. 153, this Term; cf. infra, pp. 87-92.

⁴⁸ Parmalee v. Morris, 218 Mich. 625; Los Angeles Inv. Co. v. Gary, 181 Cal. 680, 683-684; Queensborough Land Co. v. Cazeaux, 136 La. 724, 728.

⁴⁹ Koehler v. Rowland, 275 Mo. 573, 585-586.

⁵⁰ See supra, p. 33, infra, pp. 78-80.

⁵¹ The notable exceptions are the opinion of J. Traynor, concurring in Fairchild v. Raines, 24 Cal. 2d 818, 832, and of J. Edgerton, dissenting below in Nos. 290 and 291, and in Mays v. Burgess, 147 F. 2d 865, 876, 152 F 2d 123, 125. In Porter v. Johnson, 232 Mo. App. 1150, the court specifically refused to consider such factors as bearing upon the right to equitable relief. To the same effect see Burkhardt v. Lofton, 63 Cal. App. 2d 230, 239-240; Stone v. Jones, 66 Cal. App. 2d 264, 269-270.

⁵² See e.g., Koehler v. Rowland, 275 Mo. 573, 585-586; Chandler v. Ziegler, 88 Colo. 1, 5-6.

⁵³ Clark v. Vaughn, 131 Kan. 438; Hundley v. Gorewitz, 132 F. 2d 23 (App. D. C.); Gospel Spreading Ass'n., Inc. v. Bennetts, 147 F. 2d 878 (App. D. C.).

⁵⁴ Grady v. Garland, 89 F. 2d 817 (App. D. C.); Mays v. Burgess, 152 F. 2d 123 (App. D. C.); Porter v. Johnson, 232 Mo. App. 1150, 1158; Fairchild v. Raines, 24 Cal. 2d 818, 827-828.

⁵⁵ 245 U. S. 60, 1917.

⁵⁶ 273 U. S. 668, 1927.

⁵⁷ 281 U. S. 704, 1930, affirming 37 F. 2d 712 (C. C. A. 4).

⁵⁸ Carey v. Atlanta, 143 Ga. 192; Glover v. Atlanta, 148 Ga. 285; Bowen v. Atlanta, 159 Ga. 145; Jackson v. State, 132 Md. 311 (cf. State v. Gurry, 121 Md. 534); State v. Darnell, 166 N. C. 300; Clinard v. Winston-Salem

217 N. C. 119; Allen v. Oklahoma City, 175 Okla. 421; Liberty Annex
Corp. v. Dallas, 289 S. W. 1067 (Tex. Civ. App.); affirmed 295 S. W. 591
(Com. of App. Tex.) (cf. 19 S. W. 2d 845) (Tex. Civ. App.); Irvine v.
Clifton Forge, 124 Va. 781. Previous to the Buchanan case, some state
courts, but not all, upheld segregation ordinances. Hopkins v. Richmond,
117 Va. 692; Harden v. Atlanta, 147 Ga. 248; Harris v. Louisville, 165
Ky. 559.

[59] 271 U. S. 323, 1926.

[60] In 299 Fed. 899.

[61] Hansberry v. Lee, 311 U. S. 32, the other case in this Court stemming
from a racial covenant, was decided on the ground that the prior state court
decision upholding the covenant (Burke v. Kleiman, 277 Ill. App. 519)
could not bind persons who were not parties thereto.

In the lower federal courts, the cases are those already cited: Gandolfo v.
Hartman, 49 Fed. 181 (C. C. S. D. Calif., 1892), on the one side, and
the series in the District of Columbia beginning with Corrigan v. Buckley,
299 Fed. 899, 1924, on the other. Supra, pp. 41-42.

[62] Re Drummond Wren (1945, 4 D. L. R. 674. But cf. Re McDougall and
Weddell, 1945, 2 D. L. R. 244 (Ont. High Ct.) holding, apparently on
technical grounds, that such a restriction does not violate the terms of the
Ontario Racial Discrimination Act, 1924.

[63] Perhaps the viewpoint of the English courts may be gathered from the
House of Lord's judgments in Clayton v. Ramsden, 1943, A. C. 320, holding
void for indefiniteness a testator's condition on a bequest to his daughter
that she not marry one "not of Jewish parentage and of the Jewish faith".
The rather unclear state of the English common-law rule on restraints on
alienation, in general, is revealed in *The Modern Law of Real Property*,
by Geoffrey Cheshire, 4th edition 1937, pp. 518-519; cf. pp. 297-311 (covenants running with the land).

II: THE NATION'S RESPONSIBILITIES

[1] Address by President Truman at the Lincoln Memorial, Washington, D.
C., June 1947, quoted in the Report of the President's Committee on Civil
Rights, 1947, page 99.

[2] Letter of Raymond M. Foley, Administrator, Housing and Home Finance
Agency, to the Department of Justice, dated November 4, 1947.

[3] Letter of Surgeon General Thomas Parran to the Department of Justice,
dated October 13, 1947.

[4] Letter of the Under Secretary of the Interior, Oscar L. Chapman, to the
Department of Justice, dated November 10, 1947.

[5] Letter of Ernest A. Gross, Legal Adviser to the Secretary of State, to the
Attorney General, dated November 4, 1947.

[6] Report of the President's Committee on Civil Rights, p. 4.

[7] Ibid., pp. 67-68.
[8] Ibid., p. 141.

III: CONSTITUTIONAL RIGHTS

[1] 109 U. S. 3, 17.

[2] In proceeding upon the premise that only governmental, and not individual, action is prohibited by the Fifth and Fourteenth Amendments, we do not mean to imply that this assumption, based upon the decision in the Civil Rights Cases, 109 U. S. 3, is not subject to re-examination by this Court. Competent scholars have long questioned the correctness of that ruling.

[3] Virginia v. Rives, 100 U. S. 313, 318; Ex parte Virginia, 100 U. S. 339, 346-347; Neal v. Delaware, 103 U. S. 370, 397; Carter v. Texas, 177 U. S. 442, 447; Rogers v. Alabama, 192 U. S. 226, 231; Martin v. Texas, 200 U. S. 316, 319; Twining v. New Jersey, 211 U. S. 78, 90-91; Moore v. Dempsey, 261 U. S. 86; Powell v. Alabama, 287 U. S. 45; Mooney v. Holohan, 294 U. S. 103; Brown v. Mississippi, 297 U. S. 278; Chambers v. Florida, 309 U. S. 227; Cantwell v. Connecticut, 310 U. S. 296, 307-311; A. F. of L. v. Swing, 312 U. S. 321, 324-326; Bridges v. California, 314 U. S. 252; Bakery Drivers Local v. Wohl, 315 U. S. 769; Cafeteria Union v. Angelos, 320 U. S. 293, 294; Pennekamp v. Florida, 328 U. S., 331; Craig v. Harney, 331 U. S. 367.

[4] Accord: Bakery Drivers Local v. Wohl, supra; Cafeteria Union v. Angelos, supra.

[5] 316 U. S. 642.

[6] Pennoyer v. Neff, 95 U. S. 714; Scott v. McNeal, 154 U. S. 34; Brinkerhoff-Faris Trust & Savings Co. v. Hill, 281 U. S. 673; Griffin v. Griffin, 327 U. S. 220; Hansberry v. Lee, 311 U. S. 32, 41; Postal Telegraph Cable Co. v. Newport, 247 U. S. 464, 476; cf. Williams v. North Carolina, 325 U. S. 226.

[7] American Banana Co. v. United Fruit Co., 213 U. S. 347, 356.

[8] Civil Rights Cases, 109 U. S. 3, 17.

[9] Mr. Justice Harlan, dissenting in Plessy v. Ferguson, 163 U. S. 537, 559.

[10] E. g., Strauder v. West Virginia, 100 U. S. 303; Civil Rights Cases, 109 U. S. 3; Buchanan v. Warley, 245 U. S. 60; Yick Wo v. Hopkins, 118 U. S. 356; Truax v. Raich, 239 U. S. 33; Edwards v. California, 314 U. S. 160, 185; Hill v. Texas, 316 U. S. 400; Steele v. Louisville & Nashville Railroad Co., 323 U. S. 192.

[11] 320 U. S. 81, 100.

[12] Yick Wo v. Hopkins, 118 U. S. 356; Yu Cong Eng v. Trinidad, 271 U. S. 500; Hill v. Texas, 316 U. S. 400.

[13] 323 U. S. 214, 216.

[14] The scope of judicial inquiry concerning constitutional invasions has undoubtedly been most intense where civil liberties are involved. "Freedom

of press, freedom of speech, freedom of religion are in a preferred position."
Murdock v. Pennsylvania, 319 U. S. 105, 115; Follett v. McCormick, 321
U. S. 573, 577; Marsh v. Alabama, 326 U. S. 501, 509; United States v.
Carolene Products Co., 304 U. S. 144, 152-153, note 4. In the present cases,
where enforcement of racial restrictive covenants against individuals belong-
ing to distinctive minority groups has the effect of denying them the right
to adequate housing, equal justification exists for the closest kind of judicial
scrutiny into the asserted justification for invasion of that right.   Cf. Yick
Wo v. Hopkins, 118 U. S. 356; Ho Ah Kow v. Nunan, 12 Fed. Cas. 252
(C. C. D. Cal.).

[15] Railway Mail Association v. Corsi, 326 U. S. 88, 94.
[16] Yick Wo v. Hopkins, 118 U. S. 356; Truax v. Raich, 239 U. S. 33.
[17] 100 U. S. 303, 306, 307, 310.
[18] Strauder v. West Virginia, 100 U. S. 303; Bush v. Kentucky, 107 U. S. 110.
[19] Pierre v. Louisiana, 306 U. S. 354; Hale v. Kentucky, 303 U. S. 613;
Hollins v. Oklahoma, 295 U. S. 394; Norris v. Alabama, 294 U. S. 587;
Carter v. Texas, 177 U. S. 442; Neal v. Delaware, 103 U. S. 370.
[20] Ex parte Virginia, 100 U. S. 339.
[21] Nixon v. Herndon, 273 U. S. 536.
[22] Id., at 541.
[23] Nixon v. Condon, 286 U. S. 73, p. 89.
[24] Smith v. Allwright, 321 U. S. 649, overruling Grovey v. Townsend,
295 U. S. 45.
[25] Lane v. Wilson, 307 U. S. 268, 275.

[26] *Missouri ex rel. Gaines* v. *Canada,* 305 U. S. 337, it was assumed
(p. 344) that the State fulfills its obligation by furnishing "equal facilities
in separate schools."   It may be observed, however, that this Court has never
had occasion to rule directly on the question whether compulsory segregation
in education, even where substantially equal facilities are afforded, is a denial
of rights under the Fourteenth Amendment.   The *Canada* case does not so
rule, for it was held that the petitioner was entitled to be admitted to the
law school of the state university, no other proper revision for his legal
training having been made.   (The Missouri court, however, interpreted the
mandate as being fulfilled by furnishing separate and equal facilities. *State*
v. *Canada,* 344 Mo. 1238.)   In other instances, also, this Court was not
required to consider the precise point.   In *Gong Lum* v. *Rice,* 275 U. S. 78,
it was held that equal protection was not deprived in classifying a Chinese
child as "colored" and in compelling the child to attend a school for other
colored persons.   The issue whether any segregation would be valid does not
seem to have been directly raised, although its validity was assumed by the
Court. *Cummings* v. *Board of Education,* 175 U. S. 528, held that where
separate high school facilities for colored children had been abandoned, an
injunction to restrain collection of local taxes was not proper. *Berea College*
v. *Kentucky,* 211 U. S. 45, involved a state statute which prohibited any

person, corporation or association from receiving both Negro and white persons as pupils for instruction. The decision was limited to holding the statute valid as applied to a domestic corporation whose corporate power could be defined by the state. Whether a person or association could be so prohibited from teaching or whether a pupil could claim an unlawful discrimination was not decided. See, however, *Meyer* v. *Nebraska,* 262 U. S. 390, where the defendant was convicted for having taught the German language in a parochial school under a state statute which forbade the instruction of any language except English to children in primary schools. The right of the teacher to instruct was held to be a liberty protected by the due process clause which the Court concluded was violated by the statute. Accord: *Bartels* v. *Iowa,* 262 U. S. 404. See also, *Pierce* v. *Society of Sisters,* 268 U. S. 510, holding invalid a statute imposing compulsory attendance at a public primary school. The legislation was viewed as an infringement of the liberties of parents to direct the education of their children and was held to be an unwarranted interference with the right of a private school to secure pupils for instruction.

Plessy v. *Ferguson,* 163 U. S. 537, does not, it is believed, decide the issue, for, assuming that equal though segregated travel facilities may meet the requirements of the Constitution, it does not follow that the same is true of education where the very fact of segregation may, itself, result in inequalities of the opportunity to learn, which depends not only on instruction but on the association with fellow pupils.

[27] Plessy v. Ferguson, 163 U. S. 537.

[28] McCabe v. Atchison, Topeka & Santa Fe Railway Co., 235 U. S. 151, 160-162.

[29] Mitchell v. United States, 313 U. S. 80, 94.

[30] Yick Wo v. Hopkins, 118 U. S. 356; Truax v. Raich, 239 U. S. 33.

[31] 118 U. S. at 374.

[32] 239 U. S. at 41.

[33] 271 U. S. 500.

[34] Act of August 29, 1916, c. 416, sec. 3, 39 Stat. 546.

[35] 245 U. S. 60.

[36] The case was argued April 10 and 11, 1916; was restored to the docket for reargument on April 17, 1916; was reargued April 27, 1917; and was decided November 5, 1917.

[37] The contract specifically provided that the purchaser was not to be bound unless the property could lawfully be occupied by him as a residence. The majority of residences in the particular block were occupied by white persons, and the purchaser would have not been bound under the contract unless the ordinance was held invalid (245 U. S. 69-70).

[38] 245 U. S. at 74.

[39] Id., at 82.

[40] See Euclid v. Ambler Realty Co., 272 U. S. 365, 395.

⁴¹ Referring to the provisions of Rev. Stat. § 1978, c. 31, sec. 1, 14 Stat. 27 (8 U. S. C. 42), and Rev. Stat. § 1977, c. 114, sec. 16, 16 Stat. 144 (8 U. S. C. 41).

⁴² Hall v. DeCuir, 95 U. S. 485, 508.

⁴³ Civil Rights Cases, 109 U. S. 3, 22.

⁴⁴ 245 U. S. 80-81.

⁴⁵ 273 U. S. 668. Reversing 160 La. 943, in which the Supreme Court of Louisana adhered to its previous ruling in Tyler v. Harmon, 158 La. 439.

⁴⁶ 281 U. S. 704. Affirming 37 F. 2d 712 (C. C. A. 4).

⁴⁷ 332 U. S. 261, pp. 282-283.

⁴⁸ Buchanan v. Warley, supra.

⁴⁹ 8 U. S. C. 42.

⁵⁰ The District of Columbia, which is subject to the legislative power of Congress, is undoubtedly embraced in the term "every State or Territory." Talbott v. Silver Bow County, 139 U. S. 438, 444; Geofroy v. Riggs, 133 U. S. 258.

⁵¹ 8 U. S. C. 43.

⁵² 14 Stat. 27. Section 1 provided: "That all persons born in the United States and not subject to any foreign power, excluding Indians not taxed, are hereby declared to be citizens of the United States; and such citizens, of every race and color, without regard to any previous condition of slavery or involuntary servitude, except as a punishment for crime whereof the party shall have been duly convicted, shall have the same right, in every State and Territory in the United States, to make and enforce contracts, to sue, be parties, and give evidence, to inherit, purchase, lease, sell, hold, and convey real and personal property, and to full and equal benefit of all laws and proceedings for the security of person and property, as is enjoyed by white citizens, and shall be subject to like punishment, pains, and penalties, and to none other, any law, statute, ordinance, regulation, or custom, to the contrary notwithstanding."

⁵³ See *Adoption of the Fourteenth Amendment,* by Horace Flack, 1908, pp. 19-40.

⁵⁴ Strauder v. West Virginia, 100 U. S. 303, 311-312; Virginia v. Rives, 100 U. S. 313, 317-318; Ex parte Virginia, 100 U. S. 339, 364-365; Civil Rights Cases, 109 U. S. 3, 16-17, 22; Buchanan v. Warley, 245 U. S. 60, 78.

⁵⁵ Section 1977 (8 U. S. C. 41) provides: "All persons within the jurisdiction of the United States shall have the same right in every State and Territory to make and enforce contracts, to sue, be parties, give evidence, and to the full and equal benefit of all laws and proceedings for the security of persons and property as is enjoyed by white citizens, and shall be subject to like punishment, pains, penalties, taxes, licenses, and exactions of every kind, and to no other."

⁵⁶ Ibid.

⁵⁷ 239 U. S. 33, 41.

[58] Block v. Hirsh, 256 U. S. 135, 156; and see Bowles v. Willingham, 321 U. S. 503.

[59] 257 U. S. 312, 332.

[60] 316 U. S. 400, 406.

[61] 100 U. S. 303, 307.

[62] R. S., § 1977, c. 114, sec. 16, 16 Stat. 144.

[63] 321 U. S. 1.

[64] 321 U. S. at 8.

[65] Block v. Hirsh, 256 U. S. 135, 155.

[66] Cf. East New York Bank v. Hahn, 326 U. S., 230, 232.

[67] 326 U. S. 501.

[68] 326 U. S. at 506. Cf. Martin v. Struthers, 319 U. S. 141, 148.

[69] Ibid.

[70] 326 U. S. at 507.

[71] Nixon v. Condon, 286 U. S. 73, 88.

[72] 245 U. S. 60.

[73] 245 U. S. at 74.

[74] Id. at 81.

[75] Id. at 82.

[76] 245 U .S. at 74, 79.

[77] 314 U. S. 252, 261.

[78] Cantwell v. Connecticut, 310 U. S. 296, 307-308.

[79] 310 U. S. at 308.

[80] 271 U. S. 323.

[81] 299 Fed. 899.

[82] Civil Rights Cases, 109 U. S. 3, 11; Virginia v. Rives, 100 U. S. 313, 318; United States v. Harris, 106 U. S. 629, 639; Talton v. Mayes, 163 U. S. 376, 383; Hodges v. United States, 203 U. S. 1, 16, 18.

[83] 271 U. S. at 331.

[84] 245 U. S. 60.

[85] 271 U. S. at 331-32.

IV: PUBLIC POLICY CONSIDERATIONS

[1] 271 U. S. 323.

[2] "We cannot determine upon the merits the contentions earnestly pressed by the defendants in this court that the indenture is not only void because contrary to public policy, but is also of such a discriminatory character that a court of equity will not lend its aid by enforcing the specific performance of the covenant." 271 U. S. at 332.

[3] License Tax Cases, 5 Wall. 462, 469.

[4] See St. Louis Mining Co. v. Montana Mining Co., 171 U. S. 650, 654-655, "in which this Court treated as raising a federal question a contention based upon "The public policy of the Government." This Court has recog-

nized the existence of "those areas of judicial decision within which the policy of the law is so dominated by the sweep of federal statutes that legal relations which they effect must be deemed governed by federal law having its source in those statutes, rather than by local law." Sola Electric Co. v. Jefferson Co., 317 U. S. 173, 176, and cases there cited.

To the extent that an argument based on "public policy" is another way of saying that Congress has done implicitly what it might have done explicitly, we recognize the necessity of establishing the power of Congress in this field. We believe, however, that the Congressional power expressly to implement the guaranties contained in the Fourteenth and Fifth Amendments by proscribing the enforcement of racial restrictive covenants is too clear to require discussion.

[5] Muschany v. United States, 324 U. S. 49, 66.

[6] R. S. 1977 and 1978, 8 U. S. C. 41 and 42 and R. S. 1078, 28 U. S. C. 292, prohibiting the exclusion of any witness in the courts of the United States "on account of color."

[7] R. S. 2302, 43 U. S. C. 184.

[8] R. S. 2004, 8 U. S. C. 31.

[9] 18 Stat. 336, Section 4, 8 U. S. C. 44.

[10] Section 19 of the Criminal Code, 18 U. S. C. 51, as construed in United States v. Morris, 125 Fed. 322 (E. D. Ark.).

[11] Act of June 28, 1941, 55 Stat. 361, 362, 42 U. S. C., Supp. V, 1533 (no discrimination in determining need for public works). See also 40 Stat. 1189, 1201. Relief generally: 48 Stat. 22, 23; 50 Stat. 352, 357; 53 Stat. 1147, 1148, 18 U. S. C. 61c; 53 Stat. 927, 937; 54 Stat. 611, 623; 55 Stat. 396, 405, 406; 56 Stat. 634, 643. Civilian Conservation Corps: 50 Stat. 319, 320, 16 U. S. C. 584g. National Youth Administration: 54 Stat. 574, 593; 55 Stat. 466, 491; 56 Stat. 562, 575.

Employment: 54 Stat. 1211, 1214, 5 U. S. C. 681 (e) (no discrimination in classified civil service); 60 Stat. 999, 1030, 22 U. S. C. A. 807 (Foreign Service); 40 Stat. 1189, 1201 (expenditure of funds for public roads).

[12] Congress banned discrimination because of "race, creed, or color" in the administration of the civilian pilot training and the nurses training programs. 53 Stat. 855, 856, 49 U. S. C. 752; 57 Stat. 153, 50 U. S. C. App. 1451.

[13] Executive Order No. 8802, June 25, 1941, 6 F. R. 3109.

[14] Executive Order No. 2000, July 28, 1914; Executive Order No. 7915, June 24, 1938 (3 F. R. 1519); Executive Order No. 8587, November 7, 1940 (5 F. R. 4445).

[15] Executive Order No. 9346, May 27, 1943 (8 F. R. 7183).

[16] House Doc. No. 377, 78th Cong., 2d sess., p. 7.

[17] Address of President Truman, June 29, 1947, 38th Annual Conference of the National Association for the Advancement of Colored People, 93 Cong. Rec. A-3505.

[18] 59 Stat. 1033.

[19] 59 Stat. 1213.

[20] 59 Stat. 1035.

[21] 59 Stat. 1045-6.

[22] 59 Stat. 1046.

[23] *United Nations General Assembly Journal*, 1st Sess., No. 75, Supp. A-64, p. 957.

[24] No. 51.

[25] *Dept. of State Bulletins*, March 4, March 18, 1945, pp. 347, 451; Report of the Delegation of the U. S. A. to the Inter-American Conference on Problems of War and Peace, Mexico City, February 21-March 8, 1945, at pp. 24, 120.

[26] No. 41.

[27] Report of the Delegation of the U. S. A., supra. at p. 109.

[28] *Dept. of State Bulletin*, March 11, 1945, p. 399.

[29] *Documents on American Foreign Relations*, Vol. 1, 1938-1939, World Peace Foundation, at p. 49.

[30] Beasley v. Texas & Pacific Railway Co., 191 U. S. 492, 497, 498.

[31] Re Drummond Wren, 1945, 4 D. L. R. 674.

CHAPTER V: RESTRAINTS ON ALIENATION

[1] 131 F. 2d 23, 24.

[2] 132 F. 2d, at 24.

[3] 147 F. 2d 869, 871-872.

[4] Justice Miller, concurring, felt that this Court and the Court of Appeals had previously "established the law for the District of Columbia as it is set out in the majority opinion and we are bound to follow it" but he pointedly referred to this Court as "the highest Court of the District of Columbia", with power to reinterpret the applicable law. 147 F. 2d, at 873.

[5] Vol. 4, pp. 2379-2380.

[6] Comment (a) to Section 406 states (p. 2394):

"This policy is particularly applicable when the restraint is imposed on what otherwise would be an indefeasible legal possessory estate in fee simple because the curtailment of the power of alienation of such estates, totally or partially, is the situation where the dangers of restraints on alienation were first encountered."

[7] Doe d. Gill v. Pearson, 6 East 173 (K. B. 1805), criticized in Attwater v. Attwater, 18 Beav. 330 (Rolls Ct. 1853); Billings v. Welch, 6 Ir. R. C. L. 88 (1871); Mandlebaum v. McDonell, 29 Mich. 78, 96-97 (a leading American case); *Restraints Upon the Alienation of Property*, by John C. Gray, 2d ed. 1895, secs. 41-43; "Restraints on Alienation", by Sweet, 1917, 33 *Law Quarterly Review* 236, 342-348; Re MacLeay, L. R. 20 Eq. 186 (1875), criticized in Re Rosher, 26 Ch. D. 801 (1884); Manierre v. Welling, 32 R. I. 104, 117, 123, 125-129, 142 (another leading case); Mahony v.

Tynte, 1 Ir. Ch. R. 577 (1851) (exclusion, in Ireland, of "Papists", the court refusing to inquire what religion predominated in the community).

[8] See Gray, supra, secs. 52-54; *The Law of Future Interests,* by Louis M. Simes (2), sec. 458.

[9] Cf. *The Law of Future Interests,* by Simes (2), secs. 450, 456-460; *Restraints on Alienation,* by Sweet, 1917, 33 *Law Quarterly Review* 236, 243, 342-348; "The Progress of the Law, 1919-1920: Estates and Future Interests", by Warren, 1921, 34 *Harvard Law Review,* 639, 651-653; *Restraints Upon the Alienation of Property,* by John C. Gray, 2d ed. 1895, secs. 31-44, 279; "Restraints Upon the Alienation of Legal Interests," by Schnebly, 1935, 44 *Yale Law Journal* 961, 972, 989, 1186-1193.

Simes states: "In the United States the courts have been slow to approve of conditions restraining alienation as to a class." 2 op. cit., p. 300. Warren's comment in 1921 on exclusion of large classes or groups was: "Happy is the jurisdiction whose court, uncontrolled by prior decisions, or under the protection of a code provision, may declare all such restraints on alienation invalid." 34 *Harvard Law Review* at 653; "Equitable Servitudes in Chattels", by Chafee, 1928, 41 *Harvard Law Review* 945, 984, calls such racial restrictions, "a clear case of restraint of alienation." Gray, in 1895, cautiously wrote that "a condition or conditional limitation on alienation to certain specified persons can probably be attached to a fee simple or to an absolute interest in personality; but how far a condition or conditional limitation on alienation except to certain specified persons can be so attached is doubtful". Gray, supra, sec. 279.

[10] Queensborough Land Co. v. Cazeaux, 163 La. 724, 1915.

[11] The state cases which explicitly hold at least some types of racial restraints not to contravene the common-law rule against restraints on alienation are Chandler v. Ziegler, 88 Colo. 1, 4; Koehler v. Rowland, 275 Mo. 573, 584-585; Lyons v. Wallen, 191 Okla. 567; Kemp v. Rubin, 188 Misc. 310 (N. Y. Sup Ct., Queens County); Lion's Head Lake v. Brzezinski, 23 N. J. Misc. 290 (2nd Dist. Ct. of Paterson); Meade v. Dennistone, 173 Md. 295 (restraint against "use and occupancy" only); Scholte sv. McColgan, 184 Md. 480, 487-488 (same); Los Angeles Inv. Co. v. Gary, 181 Cal. 680 (same); Parmalee v. Morris, 218 Mich. 625 (same); White v. White, 108 W. Va. 128, 130, 147 (same); Perkins v. Trustees of Monroe Ave. Church, 79 Ohio. App. 457, 70 N. E. 2d 487, app. dism. 72 N. E. 2d 97 (Ohio) ,pending on petition for writ of certiorari, No. 153, this Term (same); cf. Queensborough Land Co. v. Cazeaux, 136 La. 724 (broad restraint on sale or use permissible in Louisiana).

California, Maryland, Michigan, Ohio, and West Virginia hold the rule to be violated by restraints on sale or lease but not by similar restrictions on use or occupancy; Wisconsin apparently agrees as to restrictions on use or occupancy, but its Supreme Court has not decided the issue where a restraint on sale is involved. The cases in other jurisdictions sustaining racial restraints do not discuss this common-law point. In Canada, an Ontario court has held a racial covenant to violate the rule on restraints. Re Drummond Wren (1845) 4 D. L. R. 674, 681 (Ont. High Ct.).

For a compilation of most of the authorities see McGovney, Racial Resitial Segregation by State Court Enforcement of Restrictive Agreements, Covenants or Conditions in Deeds is Unconstitutional (1945), 33 *California Law Review* 5, 8-11; Schnebly, Restraints Upon Alienation (1935), 44 *Yale Law Journal* 961, 1186, 1189-1193; Martin, Segregation of Residences of Negroes (1934), 32 *Michigan Law Review* 721, 736-741.

[12] 162 F 2d 233, at 241-242.

[13] The six criteria of reasonableness are quoted and applied in the dissenting opinion below, 162 F. 2d at 241-242; the Restatement also lists the following five factors which "tend to support the conclusion that the restraint is unreasonable" (4 Restatement, Property, p. 2407):

1. the restraint is capricious.
2. the restraint is imposed for spite or malice.
3. the one imposing the restrain has no interest in land that is benefited by the enforcement of the restraint.
4. the restraint is unlimited in duration.
5. the number of person to whom alienation is prohibited is large . . .

[14] 4 Restatement, Property, sec. 406, comment 1, pp. 2411-2412.

"A promissory restraint or forfeiture restraint may be qualified so that the power of alienation can be freely exercised in favor of all persons except those who are members of some racial or social group, as for example, Bundists, Communists or Mohammedans. In states where the social conditions render desirable the exclusion of the racial or social group involved from the area in question, the restraint is reasonable and hence valid if the area involved is one reasonably appropriate for such exclusion and the enforcement of the restraint will tend to bring about such exclusion (see Comment n ["Application—change in circumstances"]). This is true even though the excluded group of alienees is not small and includes so many probable conveyees that there is an appreciable interference with the power of alienation (compare comments j ["Application—Excluded group of alienees a very small number or not probable conveyees"] and k ["Application—Permitted group of alienees very small number"]. The violence of unpleasant racial and social relations and the stabilization of the value of the land which results from the enforcement of the exclusion policy are regarded as outweighing the evils which normally result from a curtailment of the power of alienation.

"The desirability of the exclusion of certain racial and social groups is a matter governed entirely by the circumstances of the state in which the land is located. The most important factor in solving this problem is the public opinion of the state where the land is located on the question of the racial or social group involved living in close proximity to the racial or social groups not excluded from the land."

[15] 136 La. at 727; see also 729.

[16] 218 Mich. 625, 628.

[17] In Meade v. Dennistone, 173 Md. 295, 301, the court said: "The large, almost sudden, emigration of negroes from the country to the cities, with the consequent congestion in colored centers, has created a situation about which all agree something ought to be done. In Baltimore City, with a population of about 850,000, one-seventh is negro, occupying a relatively small portion of the city's territory, though the colored area has been, in the last several years, rapidly expanding. Since the decisions under the Fourteenth Amendment, supra, no public action can be taken to solve what has become a problem, and property owners have undertaken to regulate it by contract."

See also Wyatt v. Adair, 215 Ala. 363, 366; Koehler v. Rowland, 275 Mo. 573, 585; Porter v. Johnson, 232 Mo. App. 1150, 1156-1157, 1158, 1160; Lion's Head Lake v. Brzezinski, 23 N. J. Misc. 290, 291 (quoting the Restatement); Perkins v. Trustees of Monroe Ave. Church, 79 Ohio App. 457, 70 N. E. 2d 487, app. dism. 72 N. E. 2d 97 (Ohio), pending on petition for writ of certiorari, No. 153, this Term.

[18] "Legal Restraints on the Choice of a Dwelling", Ribble, 1930, 78 *University of Pennsylavnia Law Review* 842.

[19] op. cit., p. 847, and see also p. 853. Cf. "The Developments of Restraints on Alienation Since Gray," by Manning, 1935, 48 *Harvard Law Review*, 373, 388-389.

[20] Los Angeles Investment Co. v. Gary, 181 Cal. 680; Scholtes v. McColgan, 184 Md. 480, 487-488; Porter v. Barrett, 233 Mich. 373; White v. White, 108 W. Va. 128; Williams v. Commercial Land Co., 34 Ohio Law Reports 559; cf. Perkins v. Trustees of Monroe Ave. Church, 79 Ohio App. 457, 70 N. E. 2d 487, 491, appeal dismissed 72, N. E. 2d 97 (Ohio), pending on petition for writ of certiorari, No. 153, this Term.

[21] Los Angeles Investment Co. v. Gary, supra; Wayt v. Patee, 205 Cal. 46; Meade v. Dennistone, 173 Md. 295, 305-307; Scholtes v. McColgan, 184 Md. 480, 487-488; Parmalee v. Morris, 218 Mich. 625; Perkins v. Trustees of Monroe Ave. Church, 79 Ohio App. 457, 70 N. C. 2d 487, 491, supra; White v. White, 108 W. Va. 128, 130, 147.

Wisconsin apparently upholds a restraint on use but the validity of restriction on sale has not been determined by the Supreme Court, although it has been said to be "difficult of decision". Doherty v. Rice, 240 Wis. 389, 397-398.

[22] "Restraints Upon Alienation", by Schnebly, 1935, 44 *Yale Law Journal* 961, at 1192-1193.

To substantially the same effect, see McGovney, supra, at 8-9; Martin, supra, at 737-738; Ribble, supra, at p. 849; Miller, "Race Restrictions on

References   103

Ownership or Occupancy of Land" (1947), 7 *Lawyers Guild Review* 99,
104-105; cf. Warren, "The Progress of the Law, 1919-1920: Estates and
Future Interests" (1921), 34 *Harvard Law Review* 639, 653; Bruce, "Racial
Zoning by Private Contract in the Light of the Constitutions and the Rule
Against Restraints on Alienation" (1927), 21 *Illinois Law Review* 704,
713; Note (1926), 26 *Columbia Law Review* 88, 91-92; 2 Simes, *The Law
of Future Interests*, sec. 460, pp. 301, 302; Manning, The Development of
Restraints on Alienation Since Gray (1935), 48 *Harvard Law Review* 373,
379-380, 388-389.

[23] 4 Restatement, Property, sec. 406, Comment n, p. 2412.

The Court of Appeals of the District of Columbia likewise makes no
distinction. Nos. 290-291, R. 419-420; 162 F. 2d 233, 235. The covenants
in the instant cases extend to renting, leasing, sale, transfer, or conveyance,
and are not limited to use or occupancy. 162 F. 2d 233.

[24] Cf. Steele v. Louisville & Nashville R. Co., 323 U. S. 192, 203; Korematsu v. United States, 323 U. S. 214, 216 .

[25] The restriction in Nos. 290 and 291 applies to any "Negro or colored
person", thus apparently including American Indians, Puerto Ricans, Hawaiians,
Filipinos, Chinese, and Japanese, and many other persons of Latin American
or Asiatic ancestry or nationality.

[26] Section 406 and comments.

[27] The Restatement of Property states, with respect to restraints on what
"otherwise would be an indefeasible legal possessory estate in fee simple"
(Comment a to section 406, p. 2394): "To uphold restraints on the alienation of such estates it must appear that the objective sought to be accomplished by the imposition of the restraint is of sufficient social importance
to outweigh the evils which flow from interfering with the power of alienation or that the curtailment of the power of alienation is so slight that no
social danger is involved."

[28] See also, Re Drummond Wren, 1945, 4 D. L. R. 674, 681 (Ont. High
Ct.); "Restraints Upon the Alienation of Legal Interests", by Schnebly, 1935,
44 *Yale Law Journal* 961, 1186-1193.

Justice Field's dictum in Cowell v. Springs Co., 100 U. S. 55, 57, is
often cited (e.g., in Mays v. Burgess, 147 F. 2d 869, 872 (App. D. C.) as
supporting large-scale exclusion, but the opinion in that case merely notes
that (a) conditions prohibiting alienation "to particular persons" are valid
and (b) subjection of the estate to "particular uses",—all the examples given
being admittedly "for the health and comfort of whole neighborhoods"—is
likewise permissible. Potter v. Couch, 141 U. S. 296, 315, likewise refers,
in general dictum, to restraints on alienation "to particular persons or for
particular purposes" as valid.

[29] Restatement, Section 406, Comment A, p. 2394.

[30] Cf. Schnebly, supra, at 1388 et seq.; *Real Covenants and Other Interests
Which Run With Land*, by Charles E. Clark, 2d ed. 1947, chap. VI.

[81] Meredith v. Winter Haven, 320 U. S. 228, 235; Hecht Co. v. Bowles, 321 U. S. 321, 325.

[82] Morton Salt Co. v. Suppiger Co., 314 U. S. 488, 492; United States ex rel. Greathouse v. Dern, 289 U. S. 352, 359-361.

[83] Harrisonville v. W. S. Dickey Clay Mfg. Co., 289 U. S. 334, 338.

[84] United States v. Bethlehem Steel Corp., 315 U. S. 289, 312 (dissent).

[85] Report of the President's Committee on Civil Rights, 1947, p. 91.

[86] Cf. Edgerton, J. dissenting below, 162 F. 2d 237, and in Mays v. Burgess, 147 2d 869, at 873-874, and 152 F. 2d 123, at 125-126; Traynor, J. concurring in Fairchild v. Raines, 24 Cal. 2d 818, 831-835; "Segregation of Residence of Negroes", by Martin, 1934, 32 *Michigan Law Review* 721, 724, 726, 738, 741; "Validity of Anti-Negro Restiictive Covenants: A Reconsideration of the Problem", by Kahen, 1945, 12 *University of Chicago Law Review* 198, 206-209.

[87] Hundley v. Gorewitz, 132 F. 2d 23 (App. D. C.); Gospel Spreading Ass'n. v. Bennetts, 147 F. 2d 878 (App. D. C.).

[88] Nos. 290 and 291, R. 216-219,' 227-228, 241, 260-264, 309-310, 334, 339, 340, 364; cf. Edgerton, J., dissenting, 162 F. 2d at 243-45.

[89] Cf. Fisher v. United States, 328 U. S. 463, 476-477.

[40] See Mr. Justice Miller's reference, in Mays v. Burgess, 147 F. 2d 869, 873 (App. D. C.), to this Court as the "highest Court of the District of Columbia" with power of final determination of District law.

VI: CONCLUSION

[1] West Coast Hotel Co. v. Parrish, 300 U. S. 379, 391.

[2] 245 U. S. 60, 80-81.